Knitted Clothing Technology

Other books on clothing from Blackwell Science

Knitted Clothing Technology

Terry Brackenbury
Formerly Assistant Head of Department of
Fashion and Textiles
Nottingham Polytechnic

**Blackwell
Science**

© 1992 by Terry Brackenbury

Blackwell Science Ltd
Editorial Offices:
Osney Mead, Oxford OX2 0EL
25 John Street, London WC1N 2BL
23 Ainslie Place, Edinburgh EH3 6AJ
350 Main Street, Malden
  MA 02148 5018, USA
54 University Street, Carlton
  Victoria 3053, Australia
10, rue Casimir Delavigne
  75006 Paris, France

Other Editorial Offices:

Blackwell Wissenschafts-Verlag GmbH
Kurfürstendamm 57
10707 Berlin, Germany

Blackwell Science KK
MG Kodenmacho Building
7–10 Kodenmacho Nihombashi
Chuo-ku, Tokyo 104, Japan

First published 1992
Reprinted 1996, 1999

Set by Best-set Typesetter Ltd, Hong Kong
Printed and bound in Great Britain by
MPG Books Ltd, Bodmin, Cornwall

DISTRIBUTORS

Marston Book Services Ltd
PO Box 269
Abingdon
Oxon OX14 4YN
(Orders: Tel: 01235 465500
         Fax: 01235 465555)

USA
  Blackwell Science, Inc.
  Commerce Place
  350 Main Street
  Malden, MA 02148 5018
  (Orders: Tel: 800 759 6102
                 781 388 8250
           Fax: 781 388 8255)

Canada
  Login Brothers Book Company
  324 Saulteaux Crescent
  Winnipeg, Manitoba R3J 3T2
  (Orders: Tel: 204 837-2987
           Fax: 204 837-3116)

Australia
  Blackwell Science Pty Ltd
  54 University Street
  Carlton, Victoria 3053
  (Orders: Tel: 03 9347 0300
           Fax: 03 9347 5001)

A catalogue record for this title
is available from the British Library

ISBN 0-632-02807-6

Library of Congress
Cataloging-in-Publication Data
is available

For further information on
Blackwell Science, visit our website:
www.blackwell-science.com

Contents

Preface

Very few books have been written about the knitting industry, and most of those that have are concerned with the primary process of knitting machinery and mechanisms. None, to the best of my knowledge, concern themselves with the processes and divisions that define the production of knitted garments. This is remarkable considering the major importance of the knitted garment industry worldwide.

There are no statistics that I can quote to show the balance of knitted goods versus woven goods worldwide, but it would be very difficult to find individuals anywhere who are not wearing at least one knitted article. Books on clothing technology sometimes contain reference to knitted garments produced from cut piece goods, but none appear to recognise the particular attributes of knitted fabrics and their handling to produce garments that are both special and unique.

This book attempts to give an introduction and insight into this uniqueness that affects the total characteristics of the garment from design through particular handling problems and seam characteristics, to quality control. The purpose of the book is to form an introductory text on the subject for students of apparel design and technology, and for those who enter the industry by diverse routes that do not include study of this specific subject area. The book will also provide a base of understanding for people in the retail and wholesale industries who source, buy and sell knitted garments.

Inevitably with a pioneering book, it may be said that the subject matter is too broad, and individual topics are not covered in sufficient depth. This may be an accurate criticism and may stimulate others with particular expertise to write books on specific topics that have only been covered generally in this work.

It is also to be expected that the book will require updating from time to time, for in spite of a 400 year history machine knitting is still developing and such development is accelerating. Extraordinary standards and sophistication have been reached in the basic knitting machinery that produces fabric garment pieces or whole garments.

Such innovation is echoed in fibre and yarn development, novel fabric and novel garment development, and new production methods. Just as an example, the new interest in leisure wear and sportswear of all descriptions is spearheaded by the availability of knitted fabric of entirely new construction. Recent history throws up many similar examples of knitting innovations leading to new garment concepts.

Fashion is also cruel, and to counterbalance, there are also recent examples of whole sections of the industry destroyed overnight by changes of fashion (society's demand).

Acknowledgements

I would like to thank the following firms who helped me with basic information, provided literature on their latest developments, and gave me permission to use their material in the book.

Mr A.A. Moscaroli of Rimoldi (Great Britain) Ltd.
Mr P. Atkinson of Bellow Machine Company.
Ms Janet McKay of Eton Systems Ltd.
Mr Michael Palamarczuk and Mr Michael Smith of Yamato Sewing Machines (UK) Ltd.
Mr David Dyke, Lectra Systems Ltd.
Mr David Foulkes of Investronica.
Gerber Garment Technology Inc.
Wilcox and Gibbs Ltd.
Bullmer Works Ltd.
Eastman Machine Co Ltd.
Samco-Strongs Ltd.
Mr John Bingham, E.L. Grain (S/M) Ltd.

I would like to thank my wife Maureen who, besides suffering from my withdrawal from many family activities during the gestation period, also mastered word processing to aid me considerably in completing the book.

Introduction

When most people are confronted with the term 'knitting' they immediately think of Aunt Agatha's Christmas jumpers, in excruciating colours, the necks of which will not stretch over the head. This book is not about Aunt Agatha's jumpers. Knitting is one of the most important processes for producing garments and world wide represents a considerable and increasing percentage of the population's apparel.

Knitting is used to produce garments that cover every part of the human body, in a wide range of garment types from socks, caps, gloves and underwear to upper and lower body garments varying from T-shirts to formal jackets. In spite of this range, the treatment of the fabric to produce various garments and the properties of the garments produced have a great deal in common, and it is the intention of this book to explore that commonality.

This common theme is connected with the knitted fabric property of extensibility. This is in sharp contrast to the general rigidity of most woven fabrics. The industries dealing with the production of knitted garments remain separate from those dealing with woven garments, except for the overlap occurring with dresses, suits and other outerwear garments produced from jersey fabrics.

Within Government industrial statistics the firms producing knitted garments are not classified as part of the clothing industry but as part of the textile industry. Nevertheless, in spite of the separateness of the knitted garments industry, within the fully cut sections there is a considerable sharing of production technique with the industry using woven fabrics, in pattern generation, lay planning, cutting, and production planning and organisation. Many books have been written about woven fabric clothing technology; a few mention some of the areas of overlap between woven and knitted fabric, but there are no books dealing with the particular and general techniques of producing clothes from knitted fabric. It is the intention of this book to begin to redress the balance.

There are indeed very few books dealing with the industrial aspects of knitting (see bibliography) and these tend to deal primarily with knitting machines and their products, not the subsequent processes that create garments. The primary production of knitted fabric is not dealt within this book, although an introductory chapter on knitted fabric structures is included.

There are many books covering hand-knitting techniques and the production instructions for creating garments. This is to be expected, for hand knitting is one of the oldest of man's construction techniques, and is also one of the world's most popular pastimes.

Hand knitting

Hand knitting precedes machine knitting as a technique by many hundreds, if not thousands, of years. Its area of origin and time of invention are unknown. There is conjecture that the mountainous areas of Persia, now Iraq, Iran and Afghanistan were the origin. Similar claims have been made for the Holy Land, Israel, Jordan, Syria and Lebanon; also the Atlas mountains of North Africa provide a likely site. These are all areas associated with the domestication of sheep, and the likely connection between wool fibre and knitting. Wool fibre, which is composed of protein, would decay rapidly in the sorts of climate associated with mountain areas. This would help explain the lack of early examples of knitting. Archeological investigation in these areas has tended to concentrate on the great civilisations, not peasant culture. It is also possible that references to knitting in early writings have been missed or misinterpreted.

In medieval Europe hand knitting was an important industry and socks, caps and knitted gloves were common products. Hand knitting had many obvious advantages, i.e. the simplicity and portability of the production apparatus, the lack of a cutting and making up process needed to complete a garment, knitted in the round (integral), the lack of complex finishing techniques, the simplicity of fit, and the stretch allowing various shapes and sizes of people to be able to wear one size of garment.

By the second half of the 16th century hand knitting had developed into an advanced craft, with stockings for the gentry and nobility being knitted from extremely fine silk threads on pins that were little more than fine wire. These stockings were usually richly embroidered and embellished with threads of coloured silk, gold and silver. The prices were very high and and the hose were regarded as the most important part of a gentleman's wardrobe. The lower orders wore stockings of worsted spun wool or linen or hemp, knitted or bias cut from woven fabric.

Knitting machines

In 1589, in the reign of Queen Elizabeth I, the Reverend William Lee, a curate of Calverton in Nottinghamshire, presented himself at the Court of the Queen with a request for Letters Patent for his newly invented knitting machine. This machine was remarkable in many ways: it was the product of lateral thinking in that it used an entirely different method to produce a familiar product; it employed complex interacting motions unlike any other machine in existence; and it was arguably the first machine to concentrate on increasing the productivity of a process for its own sake (i.e. the start of the Industrial Revolution).

This first machine produced coarse knitting – peasant hose – and although it reportedly caused a sensation at Court and was the object of marvel, Elizabeth dismissed the application with the following words:

'My Lord I have too much love for my poor people who obtain their bread by the employment of knitting, to give my money to forward an invention, that will tend to their ruin by depriving them of employment, and thus make them beggars. Had Mr Lee made a machine that would have made silk stockings I think I should have been somewhat justified in granting him a patent for that monopoly, which would have affected only a small number of my Subjects; but to enjoy the exclusive privilege of making stockings for the whole of my Subjects, is too important to be granted to any individual'.

Under the patronage of Lord Hunsdon, Lee persisted and produced in 1598 a refined version of his frame, able to produce silk stockings. This machine contained, it is thought, 20 needles to the inch rather than the 8 needles per inch of the original. He still did not acquire the desired document from Elizabeth, or James I, and, enticed by the French envoy the Marquis de Rosny, he moved to France with his brother James, six frames and nine knitters. The frames were set up in Rouen and succesfully operated as a small industry.

William Lee stayed in Paris, where, after the murder of Henry IV, he was declared *personna non grata*. He died in Paris in 1610, destitute and in low spirits before his brother James could rescue him.

Knitting industry

James, on learning of the death of his brother in such lowly circumstances, removed the machines back to London where the changed economic and political climate enabled an active industry to be started, with people clamouring to be apprentices to the new pursuit. James made a modest profit from the sale of the machines, returned to Nottinghamshire and with Aston, a miller of Thoroton, produced frames improved with Aston's invention of a fixed additional sinker bar.

The industry was now set for rapid and consistent expansion, lasting for 200 years until the slump initiated by the French Revolution and subsequent Napoleonic wars produced the first experiences of industrial recession (Thomis 1969.)

Such was the completeness of the frames conception that frames of virtually identical construction were still used in a productive capacity in Nottinghamshire in the 1970s, to produce shawls.

The industry during the 17th century developed as a typical Guild-organised cottage industry. The Framework Knitters Company, established by Royal Charter and based in London, regulated the industry in England and Wales but not in Ireland and Scotland.

The restrictive nature of the Guild system in respect of knitting became intolerable by the beginning of the 18th century, and moves were made to escape its strictures. Initially such moves were confined to the establishment of branches of the industry in Dublin and the Scottish Borders, but eventually they led to the breakdown of the Guild authority in the Midlands, aided by a Parliamentary sanction of 1753. During this period the Framework Knitters Company took legal action to attempt to control the trade and move it back to London.

By 1750 the distribution of frames in the country was:

London	1000
Surrey	350
Nottingham	1500
Leicester	1000
Derby	200
East Midlands rural sites	7300
Other English towns and Scotland	1850
Ireland	800

A total of 14 000 – a considerable industry.

The 18th century represented two interconnected revolutions for the knitting industry, with a subsequent effect on the whole of the textile industry. The first was a spate of inventiveness that modified the frame. The second was the diversification of the product into articles other than hose. Both these trends led to rapid expansion of the industry.

Modifications to frames

The modifications of the frames were numerous and many inventions were aimed at circumventing the inventions of others. Most of the modifications and inventions occurred in or near Nottingham town.

Among the most important modifications were:

(1) the rib frame;
(2) selection devices to aid patterned loop transfers, including pin drums and jacquards;
(3) the warp frame;
(4) selection devices to produce tucked fabrics.

These led ultimately to the evolution of warp knitting and of true twisted lace. Such expansion led to a shortage of yarn, particularly of the newly introduced short staple cotton. (The first cotton, from India, was knitted in Nottingham in 1730.)

First Hargreaves (1767), and then Arkwright (1769/72) set up their spinning mills in Nottingham. Both men were from Lancashire but were attracted to the Nottingham area by the demand for yarn, the availability of capital, the skill of local engineers and the theoretical availability of a workforce used to working with machines. What was lacking, however, was power. Watts' steam engine was invented in 1769 and was not available to Arkwright until much later. His Nottingham frames were driven by horse or mules: Hargreaves' machines were powered by hand. Felkin (1967) is of the opinion that, if the steam engine had preceded Arkwright's frame, the cotton industry would have been located in the East Midlands.

Arkwright moved to Derbyshire for water power and eventually back to Lancashire where calico and Fustian weaving expanded rapidly.

Diversification of product

The diversification of the product was connected to the inventions: sometimes an invention suggested a product and sometimes a perceived market led to an invention. Such see-sawing was to become the characteristic of knitting industry development up to the present time.

The other associated characteristic, which is not exclusive to knitting but is more exaggerated than in any other industry, is the tendency to produce multiple solutions to one problem. This can best be explained in an example. At the height of the double-jersey/jacquard fabric boom of the 1960s, every knitting machine builder produced an exclusive, patented, needle selection mechanism to carry out the function of lifting needles to knit or leaving them down to miss. There were possibly over 20 different mechanisms available at the same time to carry out the same function.

Examples of this can still be found in electronically controlled V-bed knitwear machinery, where every machine builder has progressed along separate lines and produced different machines, computers and, most important, languages to deal with the same problems and functions.

This dates back to the mechanics and engineers in Nottingham (and Saxony) all trying to circumvent one another's mechanisms to produce the same product. It is said that Nottingham was the largest outlet in Europe for powerful telescopes and can lay claim to another first in industrial development – industrial espionage! In no other industry is it possible to make a seemingly identical product by so many alternative routes.

The original purpose of the frames was to take advantage of the demand for hose. The wearing of hose (defined here as tight fitting leg covering) by men became firmly entrenched in Italy during the Renaissance, and rapidly spread to the rest of Europe. This fashion during the 15th century involved the wearing of what we would recognise as tights – close fitting garments enveloping the whole of the lower body from the waist downwards. Such garments were constructed from bias-cut woven fabrics, or leather, but it is not impossible that some were knitted. They were called 'breeches' and were often worn with 'hosen' – short socks or lightweight boots worn over the tights.

Later, as the fashion progressed into the 16th century, the hosen covered most of the leg and the breeches became ballooned shorts. This fashion was to dominate men's dress of all classes up to the start of the 19th century.

From approximately 1540 the hose were almost exclusively knitted. During the reign of Elizabeth I, richly embellished hose became one of the most important items of men's dress. Contemporary accounts speak of men spending half their annual income on a single pair of hose.

I am sure that such commercial implications were not lost on William Lee, although he was not to benefit personally. William Lee's frame was flat and could therefore only produce flat pieces of fabric. These could be shaped at the edges and garments could be built up of several pieces to produce complexity of shape, or to remove seams from awkward places such as the soles of the feet. Essentially, however, the hose were seamed together by hand and were of the type that we now know as fully fashioned, with a main seam down the back of the leg. The hand knitters were not restricted to the flat form and could produce hose in the round (integral garments).

After the wide introduction of Lee's frame, from 1620 onwards, hand knitting of hose diminished except for the very coarsest of articles. Nevertheless, hand knitting was still used to produce items like hats and gloves and possibly seamen's jumpers.

Tradition has it that with the break-up of the Spanish Armada, and the subsequent blockade of the English Channel, ships of the Armada headed northwards to round Scotland and head back for home via the Atlantic ocean. This part of the story is undoubtedly true as wrecks and founderings are reported all along the route.

The Spanish sailors carried their knitting skills with them and there are highly developed patterned knitting skills in all the seaboard places where the Armada ships could have called or foundered, including the Scottish east coast, Orkneys, Shetlands, Faroes, Norway, Iceland and the Irish Aran Islands. In the coastal ports of the North sea and North Atlantic, the upper body garments that we now know of as knitwear developed. They never became fashion in the widely worn sense of the word and were not, until recently, the objects of commerce, but they produced for fishermen and seamen essential items of protective clothing.

The product of the frame, i.e. the major output of knitting, was one type of garment – hose – until early in the 18th century when some diversifications took place; other garments, normally the province of hand knitting, were produced such as gloves, hats, scarves and shawls. These were essentially shaped garments made like the hose, either fully fashioned or integral.

There were other interesting developments. After the introduction of cotton into Nottingham in 1730 frame-work knitters began knitting lengths of simulated lacework using loop transfer techniques. Such 'point lace' created a boom, both in the commercial sense and in a spur to inventiveness.

Also over the same period other garments were made from knitted fabric, which was cut and treated in a similar way to woven fabric. Jackets, breeches and waistcoats are all items produced during this period of which there are examples in existence.

Later, in the period 1790 to 1820, such cut techniques when applied to hose to cheapen them were a major factor in the Luddite Rebellion in the Nottingham area. The knitters strongly objected to the implied productivity improvements, the subsequent lowering of reward to themselves and the lowering of the quality of the goods produced. A copy of their petition has recently been published (Knitting International) and provides a remarkable insight into the problems of the day.

The industry was also experiencing another unique event – a major change in fashion for men, away from the weaving of full hose to the wearing of trousers.

In the 19th century power was applied to the knitting machine, the first circular machines appeared, William Cotton's patent revolutionised fully fashioned hosiery production, and Matthew Townsend's latch needle enabled consecutive knitting and selection to knit and miss to take place.

The product diversified still further during this period and knitted underwear became a reality, followed at the end of the century by sportswear and swimwear (exposed underwear) followed closely by knitted outer garments (knitwear).

During the period 1880 to 1910 knitwear became established as an item of female fashion. The basic methods and division of production were established during this period and are still with us today. These basic methods are:

(1) *Fully fashioned*   Knitting shaped portions of fabric in the flat;
(2) *Cut stitch shaped*   Knitting of made to size portions of fabric, with some shaping introduced by changing of stitches;
(3) *Fully cut knitted piece goods*   Lengths of fabric from which garments are cut *en masse*;
(4) *Integrally knitted*   The shape is generated in the round during knitting, leaving little or no seaming.

Twentieth century developments

Development in the 20th century has largely involved increasing the productivity of knitting machines and making them more versatile in their patterning scope. The knitted garment is now established as part of everyday dress and most people, irrespective of age or gender, are usually wearing two or more knitted garments most of the time.

Fashion or society in its cycles sometimes decrees that knitted garments are the main form of clothing for females. The polyester clothes of the 1960s and early 1970s are an example, and the knitwear-dominated late 1970s and early 1980s are another. Such cycles in fashion prove disconcerting, if not plain disastrous, to the knitting industry. The industry contributes to its vulnerability by divisions into specialist sectors. Such sectors tend not to respond to fashion changes readily, either because of technical limitations and lack of expertise in technical and design development, or a complete failure to recognise market opportunity.

Some sectors remain aloof from fashion directly for long periods of time, but are subject to other trends. The manufacture of basic underwear, for example, trades on the basis of a utilitarian necessity but is subject to pressure from alternative production sources, being ideally located in areas of low labour costs.

Even basic underwear is slowly subject to fashion changes and sometimes itself evolves into fashionable items of clothing. The T-shirt that is currently ubiquitous wear all over the world evolved from vests.

There is currently a discernible trend in production techniques that may, over a long period, have important consequences for the knitting industry and its products. There has always been concern over the waste of raw material that results from cutting garment shapes out of flat materials. This can, in extreme cases, represent 40–50% of the whole.

It is recognised that knitting in the fully fashioned or integral modes enables the waste of value-added raw material to be largely eliminated. For a long time, however, the technology of knitting machinery has limited the range of garments that can be produced by these methods. Fully fashioned outerwear, for example, has long been confined to plain fabric with embellishments of stripes, loop transfer, tuck stitches and intarsia.

The advent of computer controlled V-bed knitting machines has changed the situation dramatically. The ability to fully fashion on a wide range of fabric types is now possible. Inhibitory factors, however, are:

(1)   the added skills needed on the part of the designer and machine programmers to cope with the complexities;
(2)   the increase in machine production time involved in making fully fashioned garments as opposed to cut stitch shaped.

This second factor is seen by most manufacturers as the biggest stumbling block because such decreases in productivity raise the proportion of the cost of the garment that is involved with the high capital value of the knitting machines and the fixed overheads. This is a highly debatable subject, balancing the savings on raw material and making-up labour costs against the loss of overall production.

The next step in this progression is to begin to lower the seaming content of the garment. Again, development of the latest computer controlled V-bed knitting machines to include fabric controlling sinkers (Stoll SMC and Shima Seiki SES) allows garments to be integrally shaped by a wide variety of methods. Such developments have potentially more savings than fully fashioned. But there are inhibitory factors:

(1) the added skills needed of the designers and programmers;
(2) the consequent decrease of production from capital invested;
(3) the argument that a fault occurring during knitting damages a whole garment.

It is my contention, however, that production will move strongly in a progression, initially for knitwear but ultimately for all knitted articles, of:

Fully cut → stitch shaped cut → fully fashioned → integral

I am strengthened in my argument in that three garment types have moved along this progression successfully. These are half hose and hose, gloves and hats.

These principles will be looked at in a separate chapter devoted to integrally knitted garments.

1

Knitted Garments

The principal feature of garments made from knitted fabric is that the nature of the final garment and the processing it goes through are affected in a major way by the primary knitting process. It is possible to have four knitted garments which look superficially similar but have been produced by four differing processes (Fig. 1.1). This chapter defines these processes and discusses the relative methods and use of them.

All knitted garments can be classified into four categories according to general production methods:

(1) fully cut;
(2) stitch shaped cut;
(3) fully fashioned;
(4) integral.

Fully cut (Fig. 1.2)

The term 'fully cut' describes the processes most akin to making garments from woven fabric. Garments are cut from piece goods fabric, laid up (spread) on to cutting tables. All parts of the garments other than the trims are cut from the lay. Each garment piece has all edges cut, hence the term fully cut.

The garments are assembled by seaming machines, often of a specialist nature, and trims are added where appropriate. The fabric for this process is invariably knitted on circular knitting machines. Such machines come in a wide range of types but are mostly classified under two headings:

(1) single jersey or plain web machine;
(2) double jersey or rib machine.

FOUR METHODS OF PRODUCING A SIMILAR GARMENT

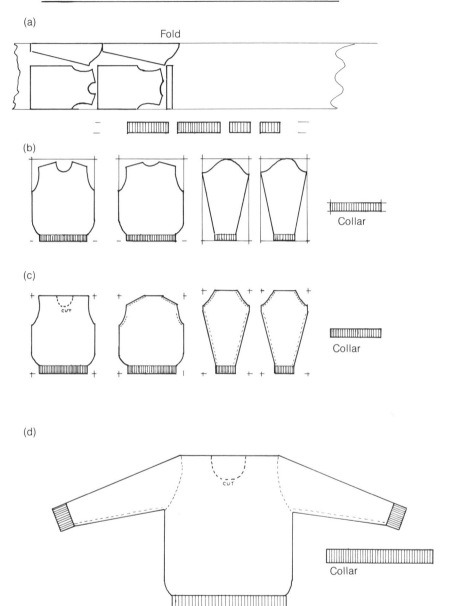

Fig. 1.1 Four methods of producing a similar knitted garment: (a) fully cut;
(b) stitch-shaped cut; (c) fully fashioned; (d) integrally knitted.

FULLY CUT GARMENTS, PRODUCTION SEQUENCE.

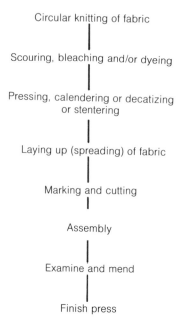

Circular knitting of fabric

Scouring, bleaching and/or dyeing

Pressing, calendering or decatizing
or stentering

Laying up (spreading) of fabric

Marking and cutting

Assembly

Examine and mend

Finish press

Fig. 1.2   Production sequence of fully cut garments.

These machines vary in diameter, the number of needles per inch/ centimetre (gauge), the number of courses they can knit in one revolution (number of feeders), and their fabric patterning capabilities. Modern circular machines are capable of extremely high production rates (300 m²/hour).

The fabric varies according to the type of garment to be made and the knitting machinery is usually designed specifically for a particular class of garment: specialist sports clothes and leisure activity clothes, jersey dresses, suits, slacks and other outerwear. Exceptionally 'knitwear' is sometimes produced.

As already suggested, fully cut is analogous to the processing of woven fabrics but there is one important distinction that influences the whole range of processing. All knitted fabrics and the garments made from them are extensible. Care must be taken with the wet and dry finishing processes to avoid stretching and thus inducing shrinkage potential into the fabric. Care must also be taken with laying up, cutting and finally the making up processes, to avoid distortions.

Making up of the garments is usually carried out with a three thread overlock stitch (BS stitch type 504), although multi thread chain stitch seams are increasingly being used on underwear, swimwear and leisurewear.

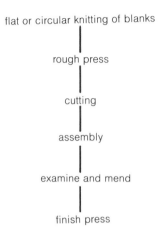

CUT STITCH-SHAPED GARMENTS,

PRODUCTION   SEQUENCE

flat or circular knitting of blanks

rough press

cutting

assembly

examine and mend

finish press

Fig. 1.3   Production sequence of cut stitch-shaped garments.

Sewing machine attachments are of major importance for speeding work times. There are general and specific attachments to seaming machines for hemming, binding, elasticating and other seam forms.

The attractions of fully cut processes are:

(1)   the relatively low costs of the fabric produced at high speeds with low labour input;
(2)   the opportunity for scale of production which particularly shows benefits at the cutting stage.

The disadvantages are:

(1)   the relatively high waste factors that occur even with small garment pieces. Such wastage ranges from 17% to 50% and is a significant cost burden on the garments produced;
(2)   the high labour cost of assembly of the garment.

Cut stitch shaped (Fig. 1.3)

The majority of knitwear is produced by this method, together with a very small production of ladies vests. The general method involves knitting rectangles of fabric relating to the size of the portions of the garment to be made. The pieces, known as 'blanks', have the lower edge of the fabric sealed with a structure known as a 'welt' that prevents laddering and distortions of waistbands and cuffs.

The term 'stitch shaped' derives from different stitch structures within the length of the blank that distort it from the rectangle into a shape associated with the human body. Commonly such shaping involves engineered rib waistbands and cuffs that restrict the lower extremity of the garment but are extensible. In ladies vests such waistbands occur in the middle of the garment blank.

These blanks require minimal preparation for seaming. Cutting involves trimming for length and sometimes for width, followed by cutting neckholes and armholes, lower arms and shoulder shaping. Cutting is still largely carried out by hand, using shears on individual or doubled pieces. Template press cutters capable of dealing with up to eight blanks at a time are also employed. Such labour intensive operations are offset by the low wastage figures achieved – 10–20%.

It pays to make the blank as near as possible to the exact size of the garment portion, or a width multiple of the garment portions. The knitting machinery employed to produce the blanks is in its mechanised form the most complex of all, although it must be admitted that simple hand flat knitting machines can produce highly complex blanks, with the 'programme' being in the brain of the operative.

There are two types of knitting machine employed: flat and circular. Both are usually rib machines, with two knitting beds and two sets of needles. Some are purl type, with two beds sharing one set of needles. Flat knitting machines knit blanks with selvedges on the side of the fabric. The blank can be any width up to the total width of the machine bed. Two or more blanks can be knitted at the same time.

Flat machines are relatively slow and even with five knitting systems the most advanced machinery makes very few blanks in an hour – 24 maximum and 12 normally. The labour of machine minding and the high capital cost of the machines feature significantly in the cost of a garment.

Flat machines vary in their complexity with the simple types being used for relatively simple garments. Most machines now are computer controlled and programmed and are built for prodigious versatility of fabric type and patterning. Other mechanical developments of this type of machinery also allow the production of fully fashioned and integral garments, although at the expense of the production rate.

The circular machines produce blanks in the form of tubes, the circumference of the tube being related to the diameter of the machine. A particular size of tube may be used to produce a certain size of garment, with minimal waste on the side seams. Various diameters of machines are assembled in a plant to produce a range of garment sizes.

Production management of such a plant is extremely difficult as changes of structure in the fabric of the blanks change the circumference of the fabric produced. An 18 in diameter machine may produce a 44 in (112 cm) width of one fabric type and a 38 in (96 cm) width of another. Inevitably either some of the plant remains idle or the plant is fully employed with added wastage of raw materials when cutting small garments from large blanks.

The approach now employed to minimise the problems is to have very large diameter machines producing large circumference tubes that are split down the side, opened out and cut into a series of widths of bodies and sleeves to fit the production requirements and minimise waste. Such a machine is the Jumberca TLJ-5E, produced in a diameter of 33 in and producing fabrics from 2.5 m to 3 m wide.

Yet a further approach is the variable circumference machine. This type still knits in a continuous revolving manner but some of the needles around the circumference do not knit. The number of these can vary and they are situated in a block on either side of a space 60° in circumference, that contains no needles. In each revolution of the machine, yarn is cut and trapped when it reaches the gap and knitting recommences on the other side of the gap. Thus the fabric is produced not as a circle but as an open width blank, the width of which can be varied to suit the production requirements, with minimal waste. The patents for this machine type are held by Mecmor who produce the Varitex garment length machine, TEJ 180, with a 33 in diameter and 12 feeders, and the TEJ 2500 with a diameter of 40 in (101 cm), 18 feeders and a maximum knitting width of 110 in (280 cm).

Like the flat machines, circular garment length machines have been subject to electronic development; computer controls have been fitted to them to handle the complexity of information required to knit a garment blank. Separate programming computers with a Computer Aided Design (CAD) facility are used to produce the tape or disk that is 'read' by the knitting machine.

The garments are assembled almost entirely by the use of three and four thread overlock machines (BS stitch types 504 and 506). Seam covering stitches (BS 602) are sometimes used on the facings or 'stolling' of cardigan and back neck seams. Collars are often attached by linked, or increasingly, mock linked seams (BS 101 or 401). Lockstitch seams are used when attaching inextensible trims such as ribbon facings, plackets, leather and woven fabric decorative portions, and tabs and labels.

Often, in the initial stages of production prior to cutting, the blanks are steamed on an open bed – in the case of acrylics – or pressed – in the case of wool and cotton. To facilitate ease of handling and maintenance of size, two similar blanks are often seamed together temporarily with chain stitch before the steaming. Heavy, rectangular, wire frames are sometimes used to hold the blanks to prescribed dimensions.

Fully fashioned (Fig. 1.4)

Fully fashioning is the process whereby portions of a garment are shaped at the selvedges by progressively increasing or decreasing the number of loops in the width of the fabric. Such narrowing and widening produces the shape of a piece of garment that would otherwise be generated by cutting.

FULLY FASHIONED GARMENTS, PRODUCTION SEQUENCE

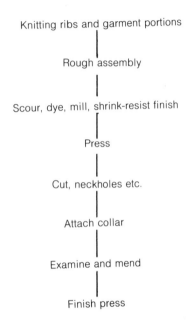

Knitting ribs and garment portions

|

Rough assembly

|

Scour, dye, mill, shrink-resist finish

|

Press

|

Cut, neckholes etc.

|

Attach collar

|

Examine and mend

|

Finish press

Fig. 1.4 Production sequence of fully fashioned garments.

Fashioning has two obvious advantages over the two previously described categories of garment making:

(1) there is little or no cutting waste;
(2) the edges of the garment pieces are sealed and not liable to fraying, so can be joined by simple non-bulky seams.

Fully fashioned garments are usually associated with knitted outerwear of a particular classical type and with a particular type of machinery: the 'straight bar' or 'Cotton's Patent' knitting machine. However, knitted underwear is made on a fully fashioned basis, although the quantity is now very small compared to that made in the 19th century. A similar situation applies to ladies hose which suffered a dramatic eclipse in the early 1960s when a fashion change wiped out an enormous industry virtually overnight.

Men's heavy rib sweaters are also fully fashioned on hand flat knitting machines, as are fine gauge ladies suits and dresses.

Increasingly the fashioning capabilities of modern electronically controlled V-bed flat machines are being used for making fully fashioned garments with scope for embellishment using a wide range of patternings. Such a use, with savings of material and making up costs, will increasingly feature as a development of the stitch shaped industry.

INTEGRAL GARMENT (1/2-HOSE), PRODUCTION SEQUENCE

Knit half hose

|

Seam toes

|

Wet finish, scour, dye

|

Examine and mend

|

Finish press, set

Fig. 1.5   Production sequence of integral garment (half hose).

Making up traditional classical fully fashioned garments takes place in two stages:

(1)   rough making up;
(2)   finished making.

The rough making up is carried out to join the basic portions of the garment together: front, back and sleeves along the selvedge. Cup seamers are used to provide a single or double chain stitch for these seams. With some styles – saddle shoulders and set-in sleeve jumpers – linking is used to join the shoulder seams, loop for loop.

The rough made up garment can at this stage be wet processed. This is carried out on the majority of garments that are single coloured, and on some that are multi-coloured. Wet processing involves some or all of the following: scouring, milling, shrink resist and dyeing.

After drying, boarding and pressing the finishing making up is carried out, including cutting of necklines, fronts of cardigans and shirts, attaching collars, facings, stollings and buttons, buttonholing etc. Linkers, mock linkers and lockstitch machinery are used.

Fully fashioned garments made on V-bed machinery are not normally wet processed, and making up is usually by cup seamers, linkers and mock linkers.

Integral garments (Fig. 1.5)

Integrally knitted garments are those that are essentially knitted in one piece with little or no seam. The archetypal example is the beret, which is knitted sequentially in a series of triangles, leaving the beginning and the end to be joined into a three dimensional shape. This principle has also been used to make skirts and jumpers and is used to produce a large proportion of ladies and gents millinery.

Another integral garment using a combination of tubular knitting and shaping is the men's sock or half hose. To shape the heel and toe of a sock, pouches are formed from extra rows of knitting.

The third common type of integral garment consists principally of joined tubes – the glove. Tubes are constructed for each of the digits, sometimes with shaped tips, and merge together into the palm portion, (also a tube). Such gloves can now be knitted fully automatically (Shima Seiki) with no subsequent making up procedures.

Integral concepts are proposed from time to time for upper body outer-wear garments, and have been the subject of patents. Inhibitory factors to their introduction include lack of competent designers and development technicians, and sheer conservatism on the part of producers.

The rewards could be considerable, saving both raw material and labour costs at the expense of lower machine output. There is little question that the electronic V-bed knitting machines in their present state of development, with presser foot or holding sinkers, are easily capable of producing garments in all the integral garment categories.

2

Weft Knitted Fabrics

It is not possible to discuss the technology of knitted garment manufacture without describing the constituent fabrics that influence the construction and properties of garments made from them. At the same time it
must be stated that this is not intended to be a comprehensive treatise on
knitted fabric.

Looped fabrics

There are three recognised looped constructions: warp knitting, weft
knitting and crochet (Fig. 2.1).

Warp knitting is characterised by the structural threads of the fabric
running along the length of the fabric approximately parallel with the
selvedge. One horizontal row of loops, or course, is made from many
threads.

Weft knitted fabrics are characterised by the structural threads being
perpendicular to the selvedge of the fabric. One horizontal row of loops
(course) is made from one or very few threads.

Crochet, unlike the other two constructions, is solely hand-made. One
thread is used which chains upon itself, and cross links are formed with
previously formed chain to generate fabric.

This book is solely concerned with weft knitting.

Weft knitting

Knitted fabrics are formed from loops. The constituent loop of weft
knitting is of the general shape shown in Fig. 2.2. It is said to have length
(ℓ), i.e. the length of the thread forming it from a to b. This is its most
important dimension and in fact decides the area the loop covers and its
width and height within a construction.

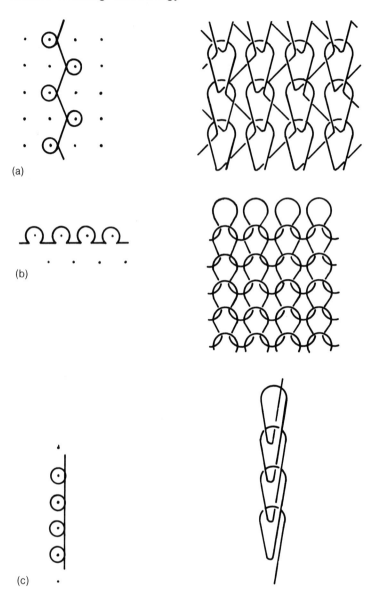

Fig. 2.1 The three recognised looped constructions of knitted fabric: (a) warp knitting; (b) weft knitting; (c) crochet.

The loop in fact consists of two bends, an upper one and a lower one, half of which is on either side of the overall construction. The loop can vary in size, that is its length (ℓ) can alter. It is rather obvious that as the loop length increases the area the loop occupies gets larger. Such a relationship is independent of the diameter of the constituent yarn, although usually within a knitted construction the yarn size increases commensurate with the loop size (Fig. 2.3).

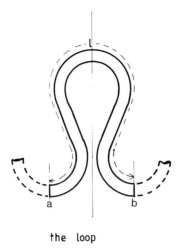

the loop

Fig. 2.2   General shape of constituent loop of weft knitting.

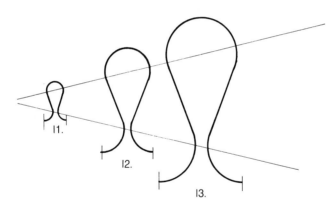

Fig. 2.3   As loop length increases the area the loop occupies gets larger.

We can describe such loops by relating them to familiar articles, so that the small loop represents the constituent part of a ladies hose or tights fabric, (loop length 0.2 cm), the medium loop the constituent part of a ladies fully fashioned classic sweater (loop length 0.55 cm) and the coarse loop a man's heavy outerwear sweater (loop length 3 cm).

Loops can be related to one another and can be intermeshed with one another to form fabrics. In a horizontal direction the relationship is a simple one of a series of loops formed by the same thread diagram (Fig. 2.4). In the vertical direction loops can be joined together by intermeshing (Fig. 2.5), whereby individual loops are connected by drawing subsequent loops through previously formed loops. The result is a fabric of matrix-like construction, having vertical and horizontal series of loops (Fig. 2.6).

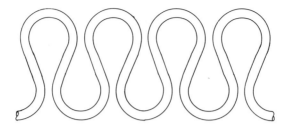

Fig. 2.4 A single course of plain fabric.

Fig. 2.5 A single wale of plain fabric.

Course A horizontal row of loops is known as a course.
Wale A vertical row of loops is known as a wale.

Plain fabric

In the simplest fabric construction all the units are of the same sort, i.e. each loop is the same shape and is pulled through the previously knitted loop in the same manner or direction. This simplest fabric is called plain weft knitted fabric, usually abbreviated to plain fabric (Fig. 2.7). Because all the loops intermesh in the same direction the fabric has a different appearance on each side. The side to which the loops appear pulled through is known as the 'face' or 'technical face'. The side from which the loops appear pushed away is known as the 'back' or 'technical back'.

Another characteristic of constructional appearance is that it is impossible to differentiate between the top of the fabric and the bottom.

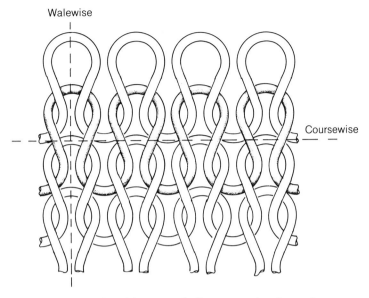

Fig. 2.6 Vertical and horizontal alignment of wales and courses.

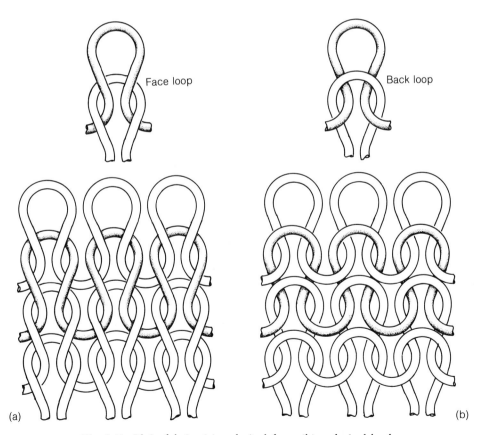

Fig. 2.7 Plain fabric: (a) technical face; (b) technical back.

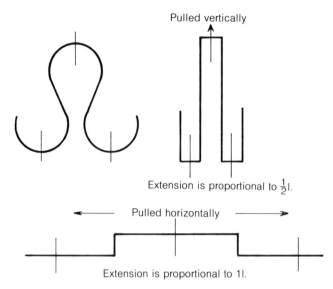

Pulled vertically

Extension is proportional to $\frac{1}{2}$l.

Pulled horizontally

Extension is proportional to 1l.

Fig. 2.8 Vertical and horizontal extensibility.

Properties

The fabric is extensible in a course-wise direction and in a wale-wise direction. However, the degree of extensibility is different when pulled top to bottom from when pulled side to side. The course-wise extension is approximately twice that of the wale-wise extension due to the degree of constraint imposed on each loop by its intermeshing.

The loop pulled vertically extends by half its length $\frac{1}{2}\ell$, while the loop pulled horizontally extends by its whole length, ℓ (Fig. 2.8). The degree of recovery from stretch is not a property of the construction but depends on the nature of the raw material and yarn construction.

This is the first of the properties related to the usual and historical use of the fabric; garments made from plain fabric are constructed so that the minimum stretch is placed vertically on the human body and arms, and maximum stretch around the body. Present and past fashions usually demand garments that do not sag readily. Periodically there have been exceptions to this usage where the wales of the fabric have run from side to side of the garment. The Dolman sweater of the 1950s and more recently is one such usage.

The Dolman fashion was essentially draped, with folds developing under the arms and around the tightly constrained waist. The draping was aided by another differential property of plain fabric: that the ease of bending the fabric is dependent on which side the bend is occurring, and whether the bend is wale wise or course wise (Fig. 2.9).

On the face of the fabric, bending takes place most readily along the wale outwards. On the back of the fabric bending takes place more

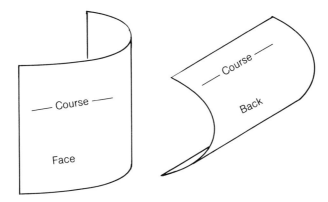

Fig. 2.9   Directions of least bending resistance of plain weft knitted fabric.

readily along the course outwards. These subtleties of mechanical performance are very important in dictating the overall appearance of a garment. In a piece of unprocessed, unpressed plain fabric, the outer edges curl vigorously. The top and bottom curl in towards the face of the fabric and the sides towards the back of the fabric. Curling towards the face tends to diminish the forces causing the curling at the sides; likewise curling towards the back diminishes the tendency to curl towards the face. A few seconds play with a piece of fabric will show this to be true. In fact in the literal sense the fabric can be said to be most in a state of equilibrium when it is in a roll or sausage form.

Pressing or other heat/water processes are used to minimize or eliminate such curling which is caused by the directionality of the loop formation. A cross section of the fabric cut vertically between wales (Fig. 2.10) shows that each loop bends in the same direction, towards the face, and is constrained in that form by being intermeshed with the loop below. However, the loop at the top is not constrained and is free to straighten, releasing the next loop, and so on, the guiding principle being that no loop or portion of yarn wishes to remain strained by bending.

A cross section through the fabric along the course (Fig. 2.11) shows a similar situation, all loops being curved towards the back. Again a release of the bending forces on the loops results in them straightening and curling towards the back of the fabric.

This property has a major influence on the design and construction of garments made from plain fabric. Obviously all the edges must be constrained in some way unless curling is deliberately desired. This is achieved by seams, welts and the use of other fabrics of a more stable nature, especially ribs.

In addition, almost all garments made from plain fabric are constructed with the face outwards as the 'effect side', with the back inwards as the 'reverse side'. This is primarily because of the difficulties of constructing side seams from pieces of unprocessed fabric. It is much more difficult to

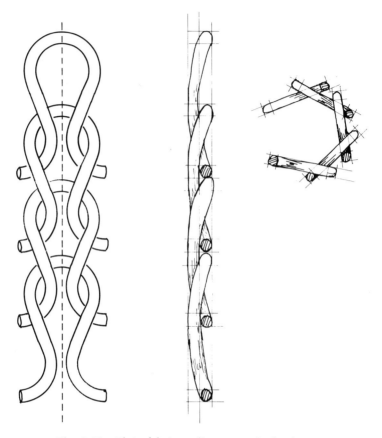

Fig. 2.10 Plain fabric curling towards the face.

uncurl the edges of fabric when they are trapped between two layers, than when they are on the outside (Fig. 2.12). Neatness of appearance also plays a part in this choice.

The constituent loops of plain fabric can readily be disconnected from the structure, course by course, by merely pulling at the most exposed thread. This can take place either from the end first knitted or the end last knitted and is known as unroving. A related disconnection of loops leading to a breakdown of the structure is caused by a series of loops being sequentially unmeshed down one or a group of wales. The resulting fault is known as a ladder. Plain fabric incorporated into garments must be firmly locked into seams, or the structure changed into a different non/laddering, non/unroving form, such as the rib of a waistband or cuff of a sweater.

All knitted fabrics, including plain fabric, are relatively thick compared to the diameter of their constituent yarns, and are composed largely of air space. Because of this, knitted fabrics have excellent heat insulating properties. However their openness leads them to being very air/water

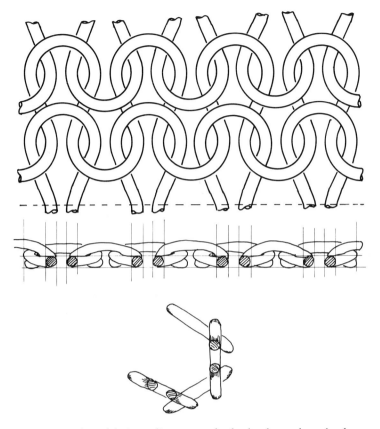

Fig. 2.11 Plain fabric curling towards the back, at the selvedges.

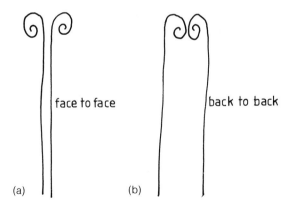

face to face

back to back

(a)

(b)

Fig. 2.12 Selvedge curling during seaming: (a) face to face; (b) back to back.

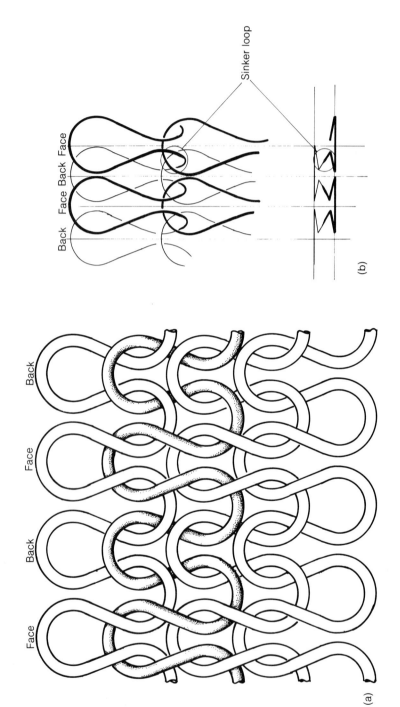

Fig. 2.13 (a) 1 × 1 rib fabric; (b) top, diagrammatic representation of 1 × 1 rib in its normal unextended state; bottom, view looking at the top of 1 × 1 rib, showing the disposition of the sinker loops within the depth of the structure.

permeable, and therefore neither waterproof nor heat retentive under conditions involving air movement.

Plain fabric is the commonest weft knitted fabric and is produced by widely different sorts of knitting machinery in all forms from circular fabric piece goods to fully fashioned panels. Other structures are covered here using the same terms and concepts as in the discussion of plain fabric.

Rib fabrics

Rib fabrics are composed of loops formed in opposite directions, so when viewed from one side both back and face loops are apparent. All the loops of any one wale are of the same sort, either back or face. The name rib is derived from the ribs of animals, whose contours rib fabrics resemble.

The simplest rib fabric is the 1 × 1 (one by one or one and one). This is formed by alternating wales of back and face loops. Fig. 2.13a is purely schematic and does not show the fabric in its normal relaxed form. When the fabric is relaxed (Fig. 2.13b) and under no strain in the direction of the courses, it collapses to a situation of alternate wales touching one another. The wales in between are hidden but show on the opposite side of the fabric.

The fabric therefore looks the same on both sides and appears to casual viewing to be composed solely of face loops. This collapse of the fabric is caused by the portion of the loops that bridges the face loops and the back loops within the structure. When the fabric is placed under strain by stretching along the course, the bridging portions are twisted into an S form by the legs of the loops. This twisting forms a storage of energy and the structure acts like a spring, quickly regaining its collapsed form when the strain is released.

Because of this, rib fabrics are used where portions of garments are expected to cling to the shape of the human form and yet be capable of stretching when required. Waistbands, cuffs and collars are typical applications, together with whole garments of a fitting nature.

Extensions of up to 120% can be obtained along the course, with normal constructions. Along the wale, rib fabric behaves very much like plain fabric, with very limited extensibility. As already mentioned, the fabric has no back or front, the appearance being similar on both sides. The fabric is also stable as a plane structure with no tendency to curl.

Other constructions of rib are possible and are widely used, such as two wales of face loops alternating with two wales of back loops to form 2 × 2 rib (Fig. 2.14). On the same basis there are 3 × 3, 2 × 1, 3 × 2 etc.

As the number of wales in each rib increases, the elasticity decreases because the number of change overs from back to front diminishes. Over 3 × 3 rib the fabric more and more behaves like plain fabric, even curling in favour of the dominant rib. Such structures are known as 'broad ribs' (Fig. 2.15).

Face   Face   Back   Back

Fig. 2.14 2 × 2 rib fabric.

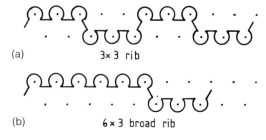

(a)   3×3 rib

(b)   6×3 broad rib

Fig. 2.15 Rib fabric: (a) 3 × 3 rib; (b) 6 × 3 broad rib.

Rib fabrics will only unrove from the end last knitted and 1 × 1 rib will only ladder from the end last knitted (Fig. 2. 16). All other rib constructions will ladder from the end first knitted. Such a property reinforces the argument for using ribs on the extremities of garments.

Purl fabrics

The simplest type of purl fabric consists of courses of face loops alternating with courses of back loops. This is known as 1 × 1 purl (Fig.

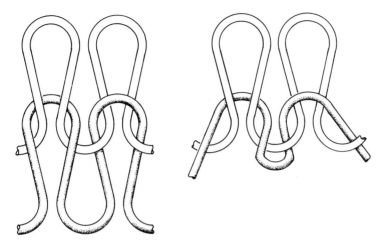

Fig. 2.16   Inability of 1 × 1 rib to unrove from the lower edge.

(b)

(a)

Fig. 2.17   (a) 1 × 1 purl fabric: (b) side view of structure in relaxed state.

2.17). This, like 1 × 1 rib fabric, is balanced: for every face loop there is a back loop generating equal and opposite forces. The fabric is stable with no tendency to curl. It does, however, have a relaxed and extended form, collapsing in a vertical dimension so that each course lies at an angle to the plane of the fabric. Looked at from the side, the fabric, and indeed each wale, appears like a concertina. The fabric therefore has a large vertical extensibility which is largely elastic, depending on the fibre used and the yarn construction. The fabric is very bulky and has excellent thermal insulation properties.

As with rib fabrics there are other combinations of simple purls, such as 2 × 2, 3 × 3 etc. These are uncommon, however, and not particularly useful.

Unlike the rib fabric, however, the classification 'purl' covers any fabric with face and back loops in the same wale. This covers a vast range of fabrics with designs in back and face loops, known as 'fancy purls'. Another term used, particularly in the USA is 'links-links'.

The three classifications discussed in this chapter – plain, rib and purl – are absolute ones and all weft knitted fabrics can be categorised into one of these classes. To summarise:

(1) Plain – all the loops in the fabric are of the same sort, face or back, depending on which side is looked at.
(2) Rib – the loops are of two sorts, face and back, but in any wale all the loops are of the same sort.
(3) Purl – some if not all the wales contain loops of both sorts, front and back.

It is of course possible to manipulate, modify and displace the loops in a fabric, but this does not alter the basis of the above classification.

Within the classification it is possible to modify the structures by various means. It is also possible to introduce design into a fabric without changing the structure, by such means as yarn type, colour, lustre etc., or by striping and plating (see Glossary). Some structures can be described as hybrids with, in particular, combinations of rib and plain to form milano ribs or ripple (bourelet) fabrics.

Others are unique structures like interlock and eightlock which fall into the rib category. Interlock consists of two 1 × 1 rib fabrics knitted in so that they are locked together. Eightlock is similar in construction but involves 2 × 2 rib. Interlock fabric is extremely stable; knitted in soft cotton yarns it is widely used in men's underwear, and leisurewear.

The main modifications used to alter knitted structures fall into three categories: tuck stitches, miss stitches, and transferred and displaced loops. It is not the purpose of this book to be a knitted fabric manual, but brief descriptions of these three categories are given here with mention of their significance in garment construction.

Tuck stitches

A tuck loop is a loop that is incorporated into a knitted structure without actually passing through or intermeshing with the loop immediately below it, but is intermeshed with the succeeding loop. Because the tuck loop is missing from the structure, the loop below it is stretched slightly to bridge the gaps. This loop is known as the held loop (Fig. 2.18). When a series of tuck loops are formed one after another in one wale, the structure distorts and a 'knop' occurs (Fig. 2.19). When a series of tuck loops are formed adjacent to one another in a course, they form a float on the back of the fabric (Fig. 2.20).

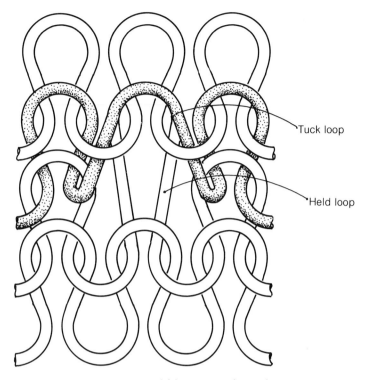

Tuck loop

Held loop

Fig. 2.18   Held loop in tuck stitch.

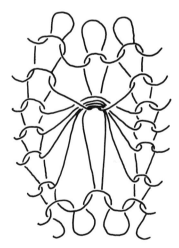

Fig. 2.19   Knop formed by four successive tuck loops in the same wale.

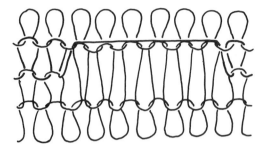

Fig. 2.20 Tuck float formed by six successive tuck loops in the same course.

One of the most interesting consequences of incorporating tuck loops into a knitted structure of any classification is the widening of that fabric. The more tuck loops the more the fabric widens relative to a similar structure containing no tuck loops. This is caused by the sides of the tuck loop, which would normally be constrained by the previously knitted loop, straightening out and exerting outward pressure on the neighbouring loops. The widening effect can be used in garments to 'stitch-shape' portions of the garment where extra width is required.

Common constructions include 1 × 1 cross tuck in plain fabric with its variations, and half and full cardigan in 1 × 1 rib fabric. Tucking can also be a colour pattern method, particularly in plain fabric fully fashioned outerwear. The colour patterning is based on the premise that tuck loops side by side in a course generate a float which is not seen on the face side of the fabric.

Miss stitches

A miss loop is generated when a loop is missed out of a knitted structure altogether, and does not pass through the loop below nor intermesh with the subsequent loop. The yarn that would have formed the loop lies as a float across the back of plain fabric (Fig. 2.21). As in the tuck stitch, the loop that stretches across the gap is known as the held loop.

Miss stitches can be used for generating structural interest as floats on the technical back of plain fabric, or as held stitch designs on the face, or to create 'relief' effects on rib fabrics. Their main use, however, is as the colour patterning medium of knitted fabrics, both plain and rib. In the simplest situation two threads form complementary loops; where one knits the other misses, and vice versa (Fig. 2.22).

More complex variations of this simple structure are used to generate rib jacquards, in which one side of the fabric contains the pattern, and the other – the reverse side – has various structures to create balance or imbalance with the face. Some of the structures can be so imbalanced (i.e. more loops on one side than the other) as to cause the surface of the fabric to bubble within a pattern. Such fabrics are known as 'relief'.

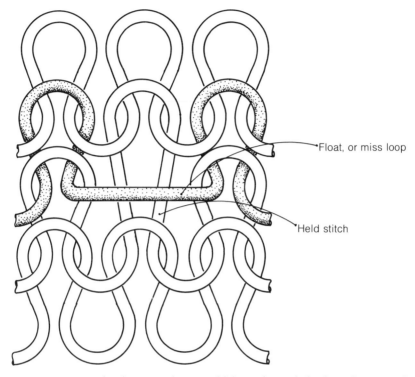

Fig. 2.21 Miss stitch: the yarn that would have formed the loop lies as a float across the back of plain fabric.

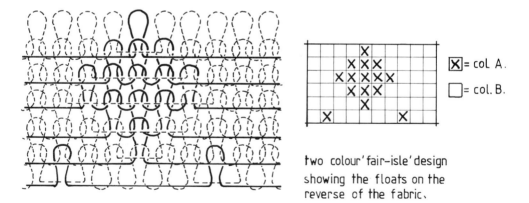

			X				
		X	X	X			
	X	X	X	X	X		
		X	X	X			
			X				
X					X		

X = col. A.

☐ = col. B.

two colour'fair–isle'design
showing the floats on the
reverse of the fabric.

Fig. 2.22 Two colour fair isle design showing the floats on the reverse of the fabric; ⊠ = col. A, ☐ col. B.

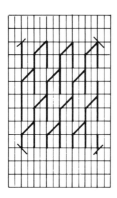 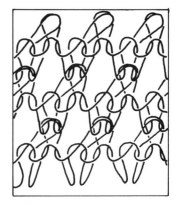

Fig. 2.23   Structure and draft of a typical lace fabric formed by transferring loops on plain fabric.

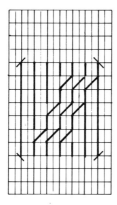 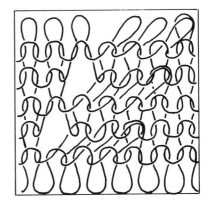

Fig. 2.24   Structure and draft of an inclined wale plain fabric.

The extensibility of fabrics is reduced but not eliminated by the introduction of miss stitches. Such reduction is considered desirable in jersey fabrics used as alternatives to woven fabrics in outerwear garments.

Transferred loops

A loop that is displaced after being formed so that it combines with an adjacent loop, or so that it appears in a different wale, is said to have been transferred.

Transferring is used to generate holes in fabric to form lace-like effects. Fig. 2.23 shows a structure and draft of a typical lace fabric, formed by transferring loops on a plain fabric. Transferring can be used to produce structural effects by inclining wales of both plain and rib fabrics. Fig. 2.24 shows a structure and draft of an inclined wale plain fabric. This is also used to produce cables by exchanging two or more groups of wales with one another.

Most structural and colour designs in weft knitted fabric fall into the above three categories of modification. These influence the nature of the garments subsequently produced from them, largely because they modify the physical properties of the basic fabrics. They also give a wealth of visual interest to the fabrics.

Other factors contribute to the complexity of knitted fabrics and to the appearance and properties that characterise them. The following is by no means a comprehensive list:

- fibre type, size, colour, lustre, cross-sectional shape etc.;
- yarn type, size, colour, surface nature, contrived irregularities (fancy yarns etc.);
- loop size;
- constructional details generating colour patterns or structural patterns;
- making a construction with specific properties of weight, insulation, abrasive or washing capabilities etc;
- wet finishes applied to fabrics, e.g. shrink resist, softening, stiffening, anti-creasing, moth proofing etc;
- dry finishes such as pressing, brushing, calendering, setting etc.

3

Fully-Cut Garments

On the whole the component shapes of knitted garments are simpler than those made of woven fabrics. This applies even when the garments are made of jersey fabrics and are intended to occupy the same role as woven fabric garments, e.g. jersey dresses.

This simplicity of shape arises out of the natural extensibility of knitted fabrics that enables three dimensional forms to be generated by deformation. Such forms in woven fabric are obtained by darts, tucks, gores etc. To illustrate this, Fig. 3.1 shows a raglan sleeve head where the shape of the shoulder is generated in woven fabric by cutting, whereas in knitted fabric in a fully fashioned jumper, the wearer creates the shoulder shape by deformation of the fabric.

Not all knitted fabrics, nor garment types, respond to this approach and this chapter examines some of the principles of generating shape in the fully cut classes of knitted garments already outlined. The production methods applicable to the cutting stages will also be outlined.

The process of cutting knitted fabric varies considerably depending on the particular branch of the industry. Practices range from the single garment handling of fully fashioned – where a cardigan front is slit or a V-neckline is cut out by hand on each garment individually, when the garment is already in an advanced state of make up – through to the enormous scale of cutting underwear from multiple lays.

Production

Included in fully cut garments is a wide range of differing types of garment, including men's, women's and childrens underwear, swimwear, sportswear and leisurewear. This range is generally regarded as within the scope of one type of company which differ largely in the definition of the market place in which they operate. A different sort of company is involved with the product range covered by the term jersey fabric.

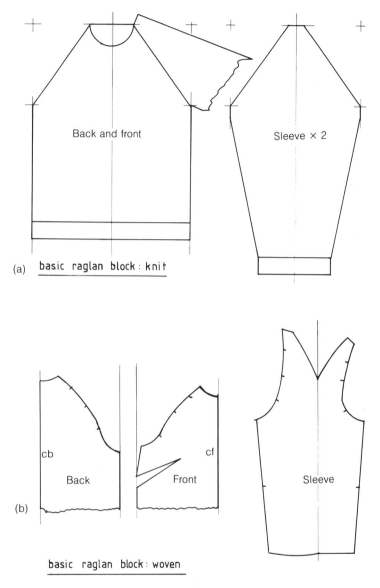

Fig. 3.1 Contrast between (a) knitted and (b) woven cut raglans.

The companies producing the fully cut garment product range are usually characterised by being vertical in organisation. The company will knit its own fabric, often wet finish and dye it, cut, make-up and market the finished product. The specific product will decide the scale of operations and the organisation of production. At one end the making of men's or children's underwear is very much mass production, with a small variation in product design and size range. At the other extreme some leisurewear is now highly stylized and subject to the vagaries of fashion. The production is organised on small production runs, quick response, a large range of designs and multiple variations within a style.

Jersey dresses, suits and other ladies outerwear garments are largely made by firms organized on a similar basis to firms making similar products in woven fabric. Some companies produce both jersey articles and the woven equivalent, although the cutting patterns are somewhat different and the making up techniques very different.

The cutting process for fully cut knitted garments is largely the same as for woven garments. The garment itself is built up of two dimensional shaped portions of fabric, which are, after cutting, assembled by seams into a three dimensional shape to fit the human body. The shapes themselves are evolved from an interpretation of the design of the garment by a process known as pattern cutting. The pattern cutter is a highly skilled person who uses a mixture of geometry, experience and creative inspiration to arrive at the forms of individual pieces that make up a garment to look like the design. Often the pattern cutter and the designer is the same person.

The pattern cutter may start with a 'basic block' which represents a simple interpretation of, say, an upper body outerwear garment and contains the correct sizing dimensions and a particular type of sleeve insertion. The geometry of the block is manipulated to generate details of shape, seam locations etc.

Trials (toiles) of the garment are produced until the correct fit is obtained. The initial garment is of course only in one size, usually an intermediate size in the range that form the market for that particular garment.

For example, in a normal womenswear size range the prototype would be designed in size 10 or 12. Other sizes would be generated by a process known as grading. This is another mixture of geometry and creativity, the object being to increase the sizes of each portion of the pattern while maintaining the general feel of the design on a variety of human body shapes. The pattern grader applies 'grade rules' that stretch or contract each portion of the pattern to a pre-determined formula.

Such stretching or contraction is not uniform in all dimensions. A given increase in body width will not be accompanied by the same proportionate increase in length of sleeves. Important details like maintaining a fit between sleevehead and armhole require particular attention.

This process of pattern making and grading results in a series of shaped pieces for each size of a particular style. Such shapes exist either as a series of strong cardboard or plastic cut-outs, or increasingly as shapes within a computer memory. It is from these shapes that a 'marker' is planned and a cutting order assembled.

The marker

A marker portrays the way in which pieces of a garment are laid out on the fabric for cutting. The marker is laid out to a particular width of fabric and within an optimum length, and may represent only one size or a mixture of two or more sizes.

The following factors are taken into account when planning the marker:

(1) the width of the fabric from which the garments are to be cut;
(2) in knitted fabric, whether it is tubular, flat open width or folded on one side;
(3) the normal length of the lay, which is connected to the type and length of the cutting table;
(4) the need to minimise the amount of waste between the marked out garment portions;
(5) the need to ease the path of the cutter blade without it getting into impossible corners;
(6) the need at all times to maintain the grain and directionality of the fabric;
(7) the alignment of patterns and checks etc.

Sometimes it is convenient to make a particular marker for a specific order, although it is more usual to standardize the marker/markers and vary the number of layers in the lays and the number of lays assembled.

The marker itself can be prepared in a number of different ways. At the most primitive the individual portions of the garments are represented by cardboard cut-outs. These are assembled on the top layer of fabric and the outline drawn round using a piece of tailors chalk. This method is very time consuming, requires a high level of skill and is open to errors through movement of the pieces and deformation of the fabric. The chalk needs to be kept sharp at all times to aid accuracy. This system is used for highly patterned fabrics that have to align within the garment, and also for short runs and prototype garments.

The hand marking system is advanced one stage further by being carried out on a sheet of paper duplicated by various methods to form repeats of the marker which can be laid on top of the fabric and cut along with it.

The marker maker lays out the pattern pieces on the paper according to a pre-determined plan. The width of the paper is the same as the fabric to be subsequently cut. The outline of the pattern pieces is drawn using a pencil or pen. To duplicate the marker several methods are available. The paper may be the top of several pieces interleaved with carbon paper, or it may be made of the type of paper that produces a line in response to localised pressure on its own surface. Carbon copies are of course limited due to the number of copies that can be obtained legibly from such a process.

In other processes the first marker is a master copy which is duplicated. Similar methods are used to those in office type duplicators, such as spirit duplicating, xerographic duplicating and pressure transfer. A form of photographic process using ultra-violet light sensitive paper has also been used. Clarity of line and accuracy are very important factors when assessing these systems, as well as the cost factor. Increasingly computers are taking over the task of producing the master copy of the marker, or are bypassing the processes completely with the aid of automatic cutters.

Marker making by computer

The past 15 years have seen a revolution in pattern making, grading and marker making in the form of computer systems. Such systems are produced by several manufacturers including Gerber, Investronica, Lectra and Cybrid.

Early systems were characterized by their high initial cost, often out of reach of all but the largest manufacturers. In the past four years another revolution has taken place with the introduction of the first low cost system, Ormus, by the British company Concept II. This system also has the advantage of being, it is claimed, designer friendly, allowing a creative approach to pattern making. Gerber have responded to this challenge with their own low cost system, the Acumark 300, and Investronica with the Invesmark DS. Such computer systems do much more than marker making. Lectra, for example, claim that their systems will perform the following tasks:

(1)   digitising and storage of master patterns;
(2)   independent input and storage of grade rules;
(3)   modification of master pattern via digitizer or colour graphic screen;
(4)   creation of new styles via digitizer or colour graphic screen;
(5)   interactive logical lay planning;
(6)   plotting and storage of markers;
(7)   plotting of single or nested shapes;
(8)   automatic lay planning;
(9)   automatic digitizing and grading utilizing scanners;
(10)   automatic laser cutting of card pattern;
(11)   automatic knife cutting of multi-ply lays;
(12)   automatic laser cutting of single-ply fabric.

Such a list covers a range of several differently configured systems; not all systems are teamed with autocutters for example.

Lectra's list could be matched in full or in part by the other principal manufacturers.

Markers are produced using computer systems as follows:

The garment portions themselves are established within the memory of the computer, either by creating them via the keyboard, digitizer and VDU screen, or by inputting existing pattern shapes using a full scale digitizer and reading off points around the pattern, or by scanning devices that 'read' the shape of pattern pieces placed on a special table. The latter system is the speciality of Cybrid Ltd.

The garment pieces can be graded within the computer system. Grade rules are provided by the system manufacturers but companies often prefer to use their own particular formulae. Markers can be planned within the computer systems via a display of a miniature length of the fabric on the VDU, and the placement of called-up, scaled portions of the garment on to it. Endless manipulation of the pieces is possible to achieve the most economical marker either by the operative or automatically by the computer working ceaselessly to achieve the best fit and to produce the minimum of waste.

Hardware and software

The minimum for a clothing computer system consists of the following items of computing equipment, interlinked and controlled by a series of software programs:

(1) The computer itself provides the facility to manipulate information input and provide rapid output. The computer also provides memory capacity to retain a certain amount of information placed into it or generated during its activities. Information can also be output in a transferable form, usually a floppy disc.

Computers are classified according to their memory handling capacity and their speed of activity. Most of those used in clothing application are classed as micro or mini.

(2) Inputs into the computer are of two sorts: keyboard symbols; or two dimensional special, e.g. digitizer or scanner. The keyboard is used to type in command functions and information in the form of words, numbers and symbols. It can also be used interactively to generate new software programmes or sub routines. The digitizer is an essential part of a graphic design system. It consists of a magnetic board which can sense the position of a pen or stylus and change that information instantly to co-ordinates that the computer can understand, locate and store.

The same function can be carried out by a 'mouse' – a small box with control buttons and a small protruding window engraved with a cross. The mouse is held in the hand, glides easily over a smooth surface via a roller in its base and transmits the co-ordinate locations of the cross to the computer without the need for a digitizer board.

Some systems, e.g. Ormus, combine the function of the keyboard with the digitizing pad so that most of the commands can be given without changing devices during working. Such a facility makes the system more user friendly and particularly designer friendly.

(3) The interaction with the computer is displayed to the user stage by stage on VDUs (visual display units), otherwise known as monitors. These are television-like screens, monochrome (black and white) or colour. Most clothing systems use two monitors, one largely displaying

commands and the other largely displaying graphical representations in miniature of the manipulated two dimensional shapes.

(4) The output device of a graphic clothing system is the 'plotter'. Individual pattern pieces, nests of graded pieces or full size markers are produced by a two dimensionally controlled pen tracing the outlines on a piece of paper whose movement is also controlled. Plotters fall into two categories:

(1) flat bed plotters where the paper is on a large table and moves in one direction when required, with the pen moving in two dimensions over the whole surface of the paper;

(2) roller plotters where the paper is stretched over a roller and moves backwards and forwards over the roller, while the pen moves in one dimension only from side to side.

Plotting speeds can be very fast. Gerber plotters, for example, can draw at 2.3 m per second.

Scanners

Some systems employ large scanners to imput patterns or block patterns into the computer system. A British firm, Cybrid, specialises in such systems, arguing that digitizing a series of existing pattern pieces is unnecessary and time wasting.

Their scanner is a box-like table 1 m × 1.7 m. On to this up to 15 pattern pieces can be laid, forming the basis of a lay plan. The individual pieces are aligned along the length of the box, as with the fabric grain. More than one arrangement of pieces can be scanned if the lay consists of more than 15 pieces or if the scanner table cannot accommodate the size of the pieces.

When the pieces have been arranged on the scanner bed, the lid is lowered and the pieces scanned optically/electronically so that they appear within a computer memory and can be displayed on a VDU screen. The individual pieces can then be reproduced in mirror image or multiplied.

Lay planning is now carried out automatically by the Cybrid computer, which is capable of working away, literally overnight, generating 'best fit' solutions that can be 'dumped' on to a disc and printed out on a miniature plotter for consideration before marker making on a full size plotter is carried out. Such a system has distinct appeal to firms that start with a stored pattern in full size on paper card.

Fig. 3.2 gives a summary of the possible outputs and inputs of a design/manufacture computer as used in the clothing industry. Not all the items listed are necessarily used on the same system.

Spreading

The scale of production of fully cut knitted garments is such that, with one or two 'exclusive' exceptions, cutting is carried out on multiple layers of fabric. To arrive at a 'lay' a process of spreading is carried out.

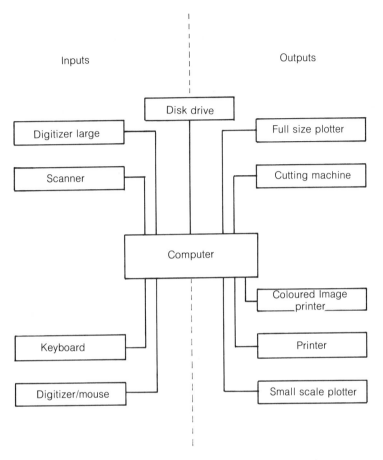

Fig. 3.2   Possible inputs and outputs of a clothing design/manufacture computer.

Spreading a lay of knitted fabric involves similar technology to that of woven fabric spreading, with one large exception. Knitted fabric is extensible and is readily distorted in width and length. Great care must be exercised in handling the fabric at all stages, whether the spreading is carried out manually or by machine. The fabric must finish on the table in as relaxed a state as possible.

Knitted fabric before spreading may itself be deformed and thus have potential shrinkage. This is a particular problem with fabrics knitted from cotton and usually manifests itself in high shrinkage by length (along the wale) in garments after their first washing. These fabrics have in fact been distorted during dyeing and finishing and have not found it possible to relax with time, or to relax in the roll form in which most knitted fabric is presented. Very stringent quality control procedures are required both to sample fabric prior to spreading and to assess degrees of distortion during spreading.

The Starfish project

The International Institute for Cotton in 1984 introduced to the industry the results of an extensive research programme into the shrinkage of knitted cotton fabrics that has 'led to a practical system for reliably predicting the shrinkage and dimensional properties of finished knitted cotton fabrics'.

This research project was given the code-name Starfish. In this research the establishment of a stable state (i.e. fully relaxed and reproducible) was extremely important. This stable state was called reference state and was achieved on all the samples by the following procedure:

(1)   wash in automatic machine at 60°C;
(2)   tumble dry to constant weight;
(3)   wet out in a washing machine (rinse cycle);
(4)   tumble dry to constant weight;
(5)   repeat steps 3 and 4 three more times, making a total of five cycles;
(6)   condition to normal regain, i.e. allow the sample to adapt to its normal moisture content in a standard atmosphere.

Further work showed that distortion of fabrics occurred during wet finishing and subsequent drying, and that differing treatments resulted in different reference states. Factors that need to be controlled during the knitting process are loop length and yarn count. In finishing, the beneficial effects of tumble drying or pseudo tumble drying, where the fabric is maintained in a state of unstressed agitation during the drying cycle, are noted.

Finally, the model relates the fabric finished state to the performance of the garment during wear and subsequent to laundering processes.

The package is marketed as a computer program and a hand held slide rule calculator. These are prescriptive and predictive, forming valuable tools for all manufacturers of fully cut knitted goods made from cotton fibres.

Hand spreading

Spreading can be effected by hand or machine. Cutting tables for knitted fabrics must be particularly wide. Slit fabric from 30 in diameter knitting machines can commonly be 90 in (2.28 m) wide and this is by no means the largest diameter. Hand spreading requires at least two people standing on opposite sides of the table. They not only unroll the fabric but constantly vibrate or shake the fabric to position it. Any localised pulling will distort the fabric which will be prevented from recovery by friction with the adjacent layers. Inevitably with knitted fabric the edges of the fabric within the lay are less well aligned than with lays of woven fabric, and there is greater edge cutting loss. The overall width and length of the lay must also be constantly checked, as distortions of dimensions tend to be cumulative and once induced may affect every layer and be very difficult to eliminate once the lay is built up. As already mentioned, knitted fabric is often processed in circular form or in slit/folded form. Both these present their own handling problems in maintaining the alignment of the two layers.

Most knitted fabric is uni-directional – there is a definite top and bottom to the fabric. (Only plain fabric of the simplest type can be treated as bi-directional.) Fabric that is uni-directional must have each layer of the lay going in the same direction; fabric must be processed from the same end of the cutting table for every layer. For plain fabric that is bi-directional, building the layers can take place from each end of the table alternately. This is of particular advantage when spreading with automatic or semi-automatic machinery.

Knitted fabric is usually different in appearance front to back, with one of the surfaces being selected to be the effect side. With fabric finished in tubular or folded form within the lay, fabric can be positioned effect side up or reverse side up. This can also occur with spreading by machine where the uppermost side changes according to which end each traverse is made from.

This is relatively unimportant with most of the common garment portions that are either width symmetrical in themselves or occur in mirror image form, left and right. But where garments are constructed asymmetrically the fabric must be the same side up in the lay and of open width finish. Such garments are, however, extremely rare.

Knitted fabric can be patterned either in colour or structurally. Stripes, prints and knitted colour designs present alignment problems both in terms of the layers of fabric within the lay and in terms of the marker in relation to the lay. Inevitably extra care must be taken and a high degree of handling skills are required to spread such a lay.

Increasingly printed pattern alignment is ignored in leisure garments and underwear, much to the relief of production managers. There is also increasing use of printing processes applied to finished garments.

Machine spreading

A spreading machine consists basically of a frame that bridges the table on which the lay is to be formed. The frame, mounted on rollers, supports and carries the fabric in roll or folded form, and the fabric is delivered as the frame passes along the length of the table (Fig. 3.3). Spreading machines vary considerably in their size and complexity ranging from simple hand-manipulated machines that contain one roll of fabric and are trundled by hand backwards and forwards along the length of the lay, to large, fully automatic, programmed machines that change rolls from a magazine and produce the correct sequence and number of different colours or fabrics in the lay (Fig. 3.4). There is a bewildering array of machines in between these extremes, with individual firms producing their own specification for machines to be made for them.

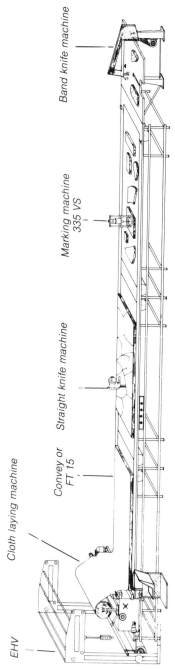

Fig. 3.3 Complete laying/cutting system. Reproduced by courtesy of Bullmer Works Ltd.

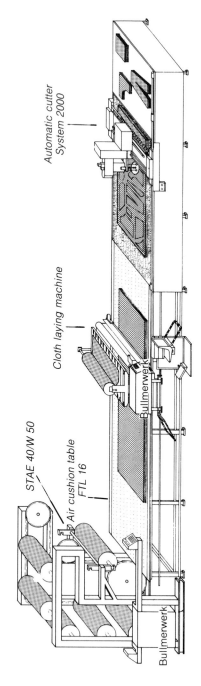

Fig. 3.4 Automatic laying and cutting system. Reproduced by courtesy of Bullmer Works Ltd.

The machines vary in their manner of traversing the length of the table. In the simplest system the frame, or carriage, is mounted on wheels that fit on to rails on either side of the table. As the machines advance in complexity and automation the wheels become driven, or become gear engaging with a rack replacing the rail. Location of the carriage relative to the length of the table becomes important, as also does delivery of the fabric with the machine positively driving the roll either on its surface or axially.

With all machine spreading it is impossible to remove the human element required to supervise the machine. Human tasks involve dealing with observed fabric faults, with rolls of fabric that run out in the middle of the lay, and, with knitted fabric in particular, undesirable stretching and skewing of the fabric.

All knitted fabrics need to be spread with the minimum of applied tension, and while machine makers claim that all their machines do this, there are some specialist machines particularly designed to handle knitted fabrics. CRA (Cutting Room Appliances Corporation) are one manufacturer of these. Their Systema series offers the ability to handle widths up to 3 m (120 in) with a load capacity of 182 kg (400 lb) on the roll. Synchronized feed rollers work in conjunction with the self adjusting dividers to compensate automatically for variations in the tension and width of the fabric. One version of the machine will handle folded fabric (cuttled or flopped).

Spirality

There is at least one other fabric distortion besides stretching, that occurs in knitted fabric and results in spreading difficulties. 'Spirality' arises from twist stress in the constituent yarns of plain fabric, causing all loops to distort and throwing the fabric wales and courses into an angular relationship other than 90°. If the fabric is retained as a tube, the spirality throws the vertical alignment of the fabric awry so that the wales lie at an angle to the edges of the fabric and slowly spiral around the fabric. Garment portions cut from the fabric show obvious distortion and are worthless (Fig. 3.5).

If the fabric is slit along a wale line during the knitting process or immediately prior to finishing, the distortion still takes place but appears as a course distortion, with the courses lying at an angle to the cut edges of the fabric. Fabrics with this problem often appear in low cost underwear and tee shirts, angled courses appearing to the consumer to be much less of a fault than angled wales.

Plain knitted fabrics made from single cotton yarn are most prone to spirality, the degree being related to the number of twists/unit length in the yarn. Such yarn is said to be 'twist lively' and, unlike similarly constructed yarns produced from thermoplastic fibres, cannot be heat set in yarn or fabric form to eliminate spirality.

Spirality is measured by the number of degrees of distortion that the

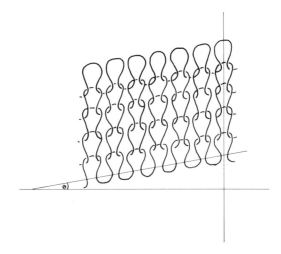

Fig. 3.5 Angle of spirality in distorted plain fabric.

fabric is away from a 90° relationship of wale to course. Fabrics of around 10° spirality are commonly processed, although acceptability varies with the quality, price bracket, and end use of the particular goods.

Resin treatment known as cross linking is sometimes used to reduce the degree of distortion due to spirality. The resin is applied to the fabric in aqueous solution and is set by passing the fabric once through a high temperature stenter (see Glossary). Besides eliminating some or all of the spirality, improved dimensional stability, appearance and handle are claimed for the process. Its main drawback is a general weakening of the cotton fabric.

Spirality is minimised by the use of doubled (two-fold) yarns, but this pushes up the price prohibitively in all but the most expensive garments.

Spirality does not occur in 1 × 1 rib and interlock fabrics, the loops formed in opposite directions cancelling out the distortions.

Another mild form of spirality occurs in fabrics produced on multi-feeder circular machines, because the number of courses knitted in one revolution of the machine distorts the wale/course relationship (Fig. 3.6). For example, a 30 in diameter machine with 90 feeders of 20 gauge will knit approximately 3 in of fabric every revolution. This will produce, if the fabric is finished 90 open width, 2° of spirality.

Usually open width finishing with the fabric passing through a stenter will correct this. Finishing the fabric in tubular form will not.

Cutting

The cutting of fully cut knitted goods covers the full spectrum of techniques available to producers of woven fabric garments, from hand shears to fully automatic systems.

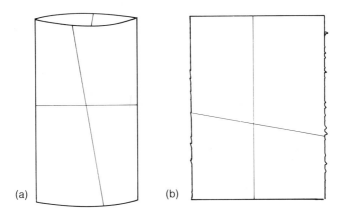

Fig. 3.6 (a) tubular knitted fabric with walewise skew due to spirality; (b) the same fabric slit down a wale and finished open width, when the spirality is transferred to course distortion.

Cutting systems can be categorised according to the cutting device used. The usual classification is:

(1) hand shears;
(2) hand held power cutters;
(3) fixed location band knives;
(4) die cutter systems;
(5) fully automatic cutter.

Hand shears

These are a widely used tool, extensively used even in fully automated cutting rooms. They are used for the following purposes:

(1) cutting exclusive garments in small quantities;
(2) cutting sample and prototype garments;
(3) cutting shortfalls in orders through miscalculation
      and rejection during production.

Hand shears vary in weight and blade length and can be designed for right hand or left hand operations. A typical pair of knitted fabric shears will have an overall length of between 20 cm and 30 cm.

In use the lower blade remains in contact with the cutting table surface underneath the fabric, while the upper blade operates above the fabric. The blades, while shearing along a line or curve, are never depressed fully until the end of a cut, otherwise jagged cutting results. In cutting more than one layer of knitted fabric, great care must be taken to avoid distortion of the lower layer or layers. The more layers, the greater the risk of distortion. Most cutters treat two layers as the maximum that can be cut.

Hand held power cutters

These essentially take two forms: the straight knife and the circular knife.

The straight knife is completely self contained except for its connecting electrical cable. An electric motor, and its associated gearing, drive a vertical blade in a vibrating manner rather like a woodworking jig-saw. The motor is mounted at the top, with a support column below on a flat plate base. The blade is mounted in front of the support column, the leading edge of which provides a slide track to guide the blade. The column is extremely thin to enable it to pass through the fabric layers after the cut. The support base rests on the cutting table surface under the fabric and its underneath surface must be made of a low friction material. Roller balls can also be mounted on the base to aid ease of movement, and at least one manufacturer (Bullmerwerk) offers a knife with blown air lift, like a hovercraft.

For safety purposes a vertical guard is mounted in front of the length of the blade exposed above the lay. Also for safety purposes some cutters wear chain mail gloves on their free hand. Sharpening is carried out automatically on the machine when it is clear of the fabric.

Lengths of exposed blade, and thus cutting height, can vary from 12 to 25 cm. The operative manipulates and guides the machine through the fabric layers, along cutting lines, by grasping a centre mounted handle. Sometimes with heavier, taller machines a further handle is mounted on top of the motor.

In many cutting rooms in the underwear and leisurewear industry the straight knife is the tool used to cut multiple layers of fabric into garment portions. It is highly productive; the speed has proved difficult to verify, with different sources giving different figures, but an average consensus suggests 5 m/min. The limitation on speed is the heating of the blade through friction. With some synthetic fibres and with cotton this can be a problem.

With some wide widths of knitted fabric, the ability to get into the centre of a lay may present problems. Often two cutters work as a team, one either side of the table. Having cut and removed the edge sections the centre can be repositioned nearer to the edge.

Circular knives

The circular knife machines vary more widely in size than the straight knives. Their construction is similar, with the motor mounted on a support column and base plate. This time, however, the support column contains the axle and drive of a circular rotating blade. It is guarded at the rear and exposed on the front of the machine. Again, a centrally mounted handle is gripped by the operative to support and guide the machine through the work. On the smaller machines the motor itself forms the handle.

Circular cutters are available to cut through layer heights from under 2 mm up to 12 cm. The smaller cutters are, in reality, mechanical shears and are used for that purpose, either cutting single or double plys or cutting across fabric at the end of each layer (ply) to align them.

The larger cutters are used for cutting lays of from 6 cm to 12 cm. Because the blade is essentially cutting on the lower quadrant of the leading edge, when cutting on the maximum depth the upper layers are being cut in advance of the lowest layer by a length equal to the radius of the blade. This is immaterial when the cut is straight, but when a curve is attempted the lower edge is following a different curve from the top. For this reason circular cutters are generally used for splitting a lay up into portions, by cutting straight lines across and, where possible, down the fabric. The portions containing several parts of the garment are then dealt with by straight knife, band knife or die press.

The circular knife cutters can operate at higher cutting speeds than the straight knives, having greater blade mass to absorb friction heat. Straight knives are heavy to push around and cutters soon tire and are prone to repetitive strain injury. Systems are available to support the weight of the cutter while retaining 360° rotation in the plane of cutting. In one example a two piece hinged arm is mounted on a vertical column at the side of the cutting table. The arm has freedom of movement above the cutting table. The arm supports the cutter and carries the majority of its weight while the cutting operative can move the straight knife freely within the reach of the arm without strain. The column can be moved along the edge of the table.

Yet another system uses a pivoted counter-balanced arm mounted on a gantry that spans the cutting table. The weight of the cutter is reduced by the counter-balanced weight, without reducing the freedom of movement.

Band knife

Portions of a lay can be moved from the cutting table to a secondary cutting area, where they are dealt with either by a bandknife or a template cutter. This is generally only worth doing for relatively small items and items with intricate detail.

The band knife employs a thin continuous blade that is driven and guided by pulleys in a 'G' frame. A portion of the blade is exposed as it passes through a flat working table on which the work is manipulated. The work itself is moved while the cutting blade remains stationary, so there is a limit to the weight/dimensions of the fabric to be sub-divided.

The table surrounding the blade should have enough space around it to accommodate the sub-divided portions without impeding the work being manipulated. As the work is moved and presented to the blade by hand, band knife cutting is a particularly hazardous task and chain mail gloves should always be used.

Fig. 3.3 shows a manual cutting system with automatic fabric laying up machine (spreader) cutting by straight knife marking with a fabric drill, and finally a band knife for the smaller and intricate pieces.

Die cutting

Template or die cutters are popular with knitted fabric garment producers, particularly those making underwear. The template knives are embedded in compressible foam plastic. The foam/knife composite covers the whole lay and eliminates the need for a marker. The fabric lay is positioned over the composite at the end of the cutting table away from the spreading zone. The 'sandwich' passes through a hydraulic press that compresses the layers so that the knives cut through the fabric as the foam is deformed under pressure. Typical presses of this type are those made by Samco-Strong of Leicester.

Die cutting is quick, very accurate and excellent for small components. Because the preparation of the die cutters is slow and elaborate, this is not a Quick Response process and is used for the mass production of slow change items such as underwear.

Fig. 3.7 shows a fully automatic system with cloth roll magazine for changing fabric, automatic spreading, lay storage on pallets, air cushion table, and a die cutting machine.

Automatic cutting

Automatic cutters are being introduced into firms making fully cut knitted garments. They are a natural consequence of the computerised pattern making, grading and marker making. Marker information can pass directly to the local computer controlling the cutting machine, or can be conveyed via stored instructions on disk.

Despite experiments with water jets, laser beams and plasma beams, most auto cutters depend on vibrating straight knives. The knife is carried in a cutting head mounted on a gantry that straddles the cutting table. The knife can rotate through 360° below the head; the head can move freely across the gantry; and the gantry can move on rails along the length of the cutting table. Cutting can therefore take place in any direction over the whole surface of the table (Fig. 3.4).

The tables themselves are specially constructed so that the surface will support the lay and yet allow penetration by the knife through all the layers. Usually such tables have a surface of closely packed nylon or similar plastic bristles (Fig. 3.4).

Spreading is invariably carried out on another table or tables, but sometimes the spreading table is an extension of the cutting table so that a flow pattern is established.

Fig. 3.4 shows an automatic cutting line with cloth roll magazine changer and automatic spreading on to an air cushion table to aid the movement of the lay on to the bristle vacuum cutting table. Cutting is with a CNC-system 2000 auto cutter. The cut portions are assembled into bundles from an end work table.

On one of the Bullmerwerk System 2000 versions, the bristle mat is itself a conveyor.

Essential to the operation of automatic cutters is that the lay remains

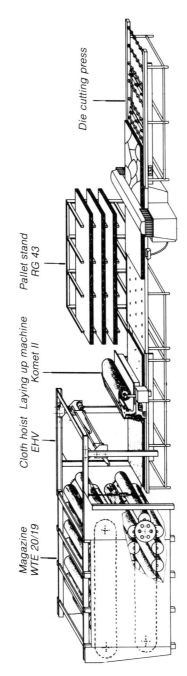

Fig. 3.7 Automatic laying and cutting system incorporating a die cutter. Reproduced by courtesy of Bullmer Works Ltd.

compact and undisturbed by the progress of the knife at high speed, and by the current of air associated with motor cooling etc. To this end an important feature of automatic cutting tables is that the lay is controlled by an under-table vacuum, maintained by very high powered air pumps.

For example, on Gerbers S-95 table for low and medium ply cutting (up to 10 mm), maintaining the vacuum on a working surface of up to 2 m by 3.6 m requires 30 KVA (kilo volt amperes). On the Gerber S-91 for plys up to 76 mm on a similar area 70 KVA is required to maintain the vacuum.

The surface of the lay is covered with a plastic film or special paper to contain the vacuum. The lay itself compresses under the vacuum and any movement between plys is eliminated completely. Cutting speeds are high. Different makers of machines quote up to 20–30 m/min. Such speeds refer to low ply heights or even single layer cutting. On maximum heights with difficult fabrics cutting speeds are reduced and on knitted fabrics are more realistically between 8 and 16 m/min.

Blade heating is the limitation on cutting speed and must be avoided to reduce the risk of fusing or scorching. The cutting heads incorporate automatic blade sharpening.

It can be argued that cutting speeds are irrelevant, and that the gains of automatic cutting lie in the ability to eliminate marker making and to change cutting, fabric type, height of lay, length and width of fabric, etc., to enable a manufacturer to engage in Quick Response.

Some manufacturers producing 'high return' articles in jersey fabrics find it economical to cut single or double layers of fabric automatically and claim that the cost is lower than hand cutting.

Table dimensions of automatic systems are relatively small: 2 m, 2.4 m, 3 m and 3.6 m are common lengths, and 1 or 2 m widths are usual.

Knitted fabrics, like wide woven fabrics, need subdividing longitudinally. Systems are available to carry this out during the spreading process.

Summary

All the cutting methods discussed are used in the fully cut knitted garment industry. All have a valid role to play in particular situations and are tools by which cutting room managers can respond to the ever varying demands of the market.

The balance between low capital cost/high labour cost and high capital cost/low labour cost is complicated by the demands of Quick Response.

In this section of production in particular, high output potential associated with high capital cost, is not linked inextricably with mass production.

4

Cut Stitch-Shaped Garments

In Chapter 2 the general principles of the production of cut stitch-shaped garments are outlined. Most cut stitch-shaped garments are upper body garments of the knitwear variety. Within this category a large variety of men's, ladies', and children's garments are produced in the form of jumpers, slipovers, cardigans, jackets and waistcoats. Most fashion knitwear falls in this category. The term fashion in this sense describes designs that are up to the minute, short-lived, appealing to younger age groups and mostly women's wear but including some men's wear. The term implies the opposite of classical.

Other garments made by cut stitch-shaped techniques are some forms of ladies' vests, dresses and skirts. Knitted dresses in particular are very fashion dependent and appear on the market infrequently.

The widest variety of stitch forms and colour pattern work also occurs in this classification, and these in fact form the main basis of a particular design. The shape of the garments is relatively simple, and while overall form in terms of the length of the garment and the relative looseness or tightness of fit are important, the main appeals are in the textile design content.

Garments tend to be classified according to neck opening style and sleeve head attachment. The latter is more important as it determines the size of the knitted blanks and the economics in terms of raw material utilization. Neck openings are regarded as a variable option that can be carried out on a standardized overall body shape. Popular neck openings/ treatment styles for jumpers include round neck, V-neck, turtle neck, polo neck and shirt collar types (see Glossary). Most cardigans are given a simple facing that varies with the nature of the ribbing or stolling used. Other designs are achieved by rolled revers and collars.

Economic considerations tend to impose limitations on the type of sleeve head shape used. With cut knitwear this limitation is mainly in the variations of set-in sleeve heads and drop shoulders. The sleeves for such

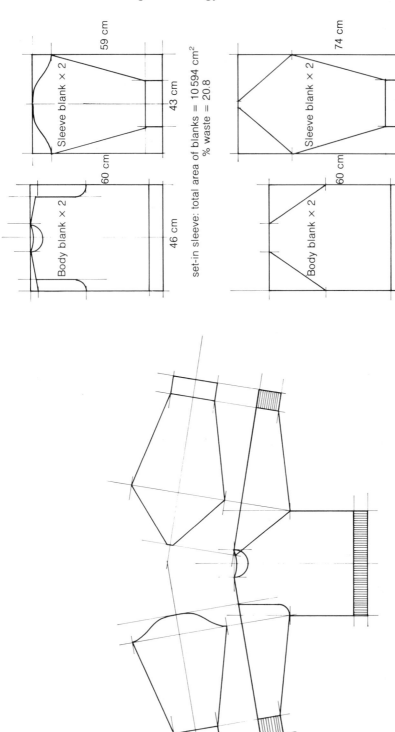

Sleeve blank × 2

59 cm

43 cm

Body blank × 2

60 cm

46 cm

set-in sleeve: total area of blanks = 10 594 cm²
% waste = 20.8

Sleeve blank × 2

74 cm

43 cm

Body blank × 2

60 cm

46 cm

raglan sleeve: total area of blanks = 11 884
% waste = 22.1

Fig. 4.1 Round neck jumper basic block with raglan sleeve and set-in sleeve adaptations, showing the fabric area required for the variation of sleeve head shape. The raglan sleeve version requires 12% more fabric.

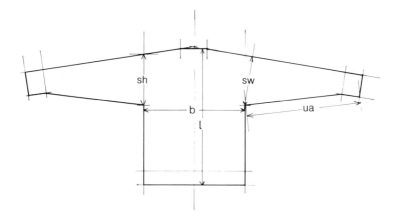

Fig. 4.2 Important dimensions in knitwear specification: b = bust width; l = length; sh = sleeve head; sw = sleeve width; ua = underarm.

shapes can be produced from smaller blanks than raglan or saddle shoulder types. Fig. 4.1 shows a comparison of blank sizes and the relative wastage levels for a set-in sleeve garment and raglan sleeved garment of similar size, shape and overall weight.

While percentage wastage levels are useful in comparing garments made from different cut processes with those fully fashioned, they are of little use in assessing garments cut from the same sizes of blanks. The raw material cost of a cut stitch-shaped garment is solely dependent on the size/weight of the blanks from which it is cut. Within the blank it is quite irrelevant whether the waste is 25% or 35%, except from a moral standpoint. The shapes themselves are usually very simple for cut stitch-shaped garments. Side body line is invariably straight below the underarm, with constriction caused by rib waistbands at the lower end; length is variable and the 'waist' can be in any position from just below the bust to below crotch level. Sometimes, when fashion demands tight fitting knitwear, some shaping from underarm to waist is inserted.

Sleeve heads are invariably symmetrical, as are front and back armholes on the body portions. The general fit of the garment over the contours of the body, and the articulations of the arms, depend almost wholly on the elastic deformation of the fabric. Darts are not generally used to generate bust shapes or upper back shoulder shaping.

Important dimensions in determining the overall appearance of knitwear garments are (Fig. 4.2):

(1)   bust width, measured underarm;
(2)   length, measured back neck to extremity;
(3)   sleeve head depth;
(4)   sleeve width;
(5)   underarm sleeve length.

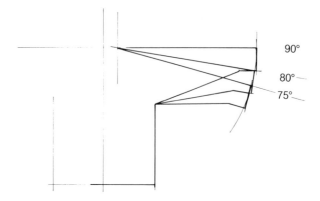

Fig. 4.3 Body/sleeve angles.

Also of major importance to the overall fit, comfort and appearance is the angle that the sleeve makes with the body (Fig. 4.3). At 90° the sleeve/body junction is very full and drapes, tending to pull the shoulder line downwards. At 75° the sleeve/body join is beginning to feel constricted. Most shoulder/sleeve slopes are of the order of 80° to 85°.

This angle can also be expressed as shoulder slope. That is the angle formed between a line projected from the neck, perpendicular to the centre body line, and the upper edge of the sleeve.

Shoulder slope = 90° − body/sleeve angle

The above measurements are the ones that are the most important in quality control procedures and are the basis for specification.

If this so far appears restrictive of shape and fashion styles, that is not the intention. It is simply that this section caters for Quick Response fashion and almost anything goes in terms of garment definition and shape detail.

Cutting

Prior to making and cutting it is normal to subject the garment blanks to an open bed steam treatment. This has two objectives:

(1)   to relax the blank and stabilize its surface;
(2)   to regulate its size and shape.

To ensure the second objective metal forms are often used, inserted into the tube formed by two flat blanks temporarily seamed together, or one wide flat blank folded and seamed, or the tubular blank from a circular machine. The blanks are then steamed with the forms in place. In the main, most cut knitwear is produced from acrylic yarns, it being generally uneconomic to cut wool, cotton or other natural fibres to waste.

Acrylic fibres are very thermoplastic and great care is needed, when the blanks are on the steam bed and hot, to avoid distorting them by undue handling. After steaming and cooling, acrylic fabrics are very stable and do not exhibit the dimensional instability of, say, cotton. When wool or cotton is used for cut knitwear it is often given an actual press at this stage to neaten and stabilize it.

Cutting is still mostly done by hand with shears on individual garment pieces. Cardboard pattern shapes are used and the cutting lines are chalked on to the fabric. Often such chalk lines are only approximate guides, it being more important to cut to a particular structural or pattern feature. It is also normal practice to cut along the wale line of the rib cuffs, waistbands or hems. Sometimes a tight specification demands that this is in a precise position, and the ribs are actually counted to achieve this.

Sometimes negative pattern shapes are used, i.e. the shape of the portion to be cut away rather than the shape of the garment. V-necks are commonly treated in this way, it being easier to align a small piece of card on what is quite an unstable surface.

The actual cutting takes place on a flat table of sufficient height that the cutter, who stands, feels comfortable and does not suffer back stress. Two body blanks are usually cut together, i.e. a front and back, or two sleeves. As already outlined these may already be in tubular form, or, if flat, tacked together. The body front and back are cut together for the sleeve insert and back neck; the body front is then cut for the neckline. If there is side body excess or length excess this is cut off initially.

To speed production, template or die cutters are used for large orders or when standardized shapes are used.

This involves two beds. On the lower one the garment portions are assembled, accurately aligned. The lower bed usually contains the cutting template, although it can be in the upper bed. The cutter itself consists of thin steel strips, razor sharp on one edge, embedded in a deformable plastic substrate. The steel strips define the outline of the garment and are specially made and assembled for each size and type of garment.

When the garment pile is ready to cut, the beds are aligned and pressure applied to force the template knives through the pile of garments. Safety is of prime importance and guards and two handed switches are fitted to prevent accidents. The device can handle up to eight pieces at a time. Front necks are usually cut out afterwards by hand. Separate machines are required to handle bodies and sleeves, and only one size can be cut at once.

Some firms use die cutters to cut single pieces of garments from blanks, i.e. front or back or sleeve. The usual practice is to fold the blank vertically down a centre line which is placed accurately on a mark on the lower bed. It is claimed that a dozen garments can be cut in seven minutes, not counting the time to change the knives. This is quick and simple as the knives merely slide off a plastic sheet, to be replaced with others.

The claim made for single garment piece cutting is high accuracy; there is a tendency for piles of fabric to distort under the pressure between the two beds.

Hybrid cut/fully fashioned garments

Mention should be made of hybrids between cut knitwear and fully fashioned knitwear. There are two sorts, varying only in the method of shaping on the V-bed flat knitting machines: press-off shaping and held-stitch shaping. The end results are the same: eliminating the cutting stage and saving raw materials.

Modern computer-controlled V-bed flat knitting machines equipped with presser feet (stitch pressers) or with loop holding sinkers are capable of knitting without imposing take-down load on the fabric being formed. This allows loops to be dropped off needles at the edge of the fabric without the fabric disintegrating into ladders and holes. Such pressing-off can be used to generate a sleeve head shape, or a sleeve insertion hole, or to form raglan sleeves which otherwise, as already outlined, are uneconomic. The pressing-off can be done gradually, loop by loop or in steps. Trimming is usually left to the knives of the overlock machine.

The held-stitch technique involves holding the loops at the edge of the knitting and reducing in stages the length of the course being knitted. No pressing-off takes place until the shape is completed and two or three edge rows have been knitted. This technique is particularly useful for set-in sleeve heads and shoulder slopes.

Such narrowing techniques can be combined with needle introduction widening for sleeves, and very large savings can be made. In spite of the obvious advantages of such techniques in economic terms, with the saving of raw material and cutting time, and little or no increase in knitting time, they are still not widely practised.

5

Fully Fashioned Garments

Shaping by fully fashioning involves the movement of a small number of loops at the selvedge of the fabric. Such movement reduces or increases the total number of loops being knitted. The terms used in the industry for such movements are narrowing and widening, and collectively fashioning.

When narrowing, the innermost loop of the group being moved combines with the loop adjacent to it. Fig. 5.1 represents two loops being moved by one loop space, thus losing one loop at the edge. It is possible on plain fabric to move the edge loops more than one needle space, losing more than one loop at the edge. In the fully fashioned industry these are known as 'needle narrowings' e.g. two needle narrowings where the outer group are moved in two needles. Such multi-loop narrowings produce small puckers where the loops combine. The number of loops in the group being moved varies from three to seven, with finer fabrics tending to involve more loops than coarser fabrics.

With successive fashioning the wales at the outer edge of the fabric follow the shape of the selvedge, giving the characteristic signature of fully fashioned garments. There is a utilitarian reason for the movement of several loops rather than just one: it allows seaming to follow a wale line throughout the garment, giving neatness of assembly.

In widening, the movement outwards creates a space adjacent to the innermost needle of the group, where a new wale may start (Fig. 5.2). The empty space, followed by the tuck loop formed at the next knitted course, leaves a hole in the fabric. It is usual in commercial practice to fill this hole by moving a previously knitted loop to commence the new wale. Such holes restrict the widenings to single needle only (Fig. 5.3).

Fashioning is not restricted to plain fabric only; rib fabrics are increasingly the subject of fully fashioning. Particularly suitable for shaping in this way are the cardigan fabrics containing tuck loops and broad ribs.

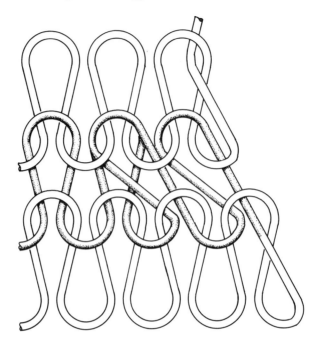

Fig. 5.1 A single needle narrowing.

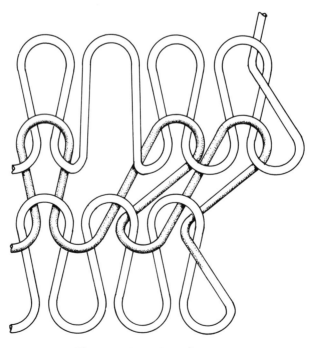

Fig. 5.2 A single widening.

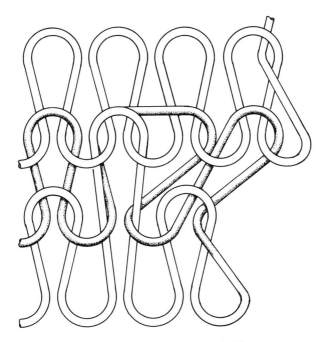

Fig. 5.3 A single widening with filling in.

Shape Generation

As already explained, fashioning involves the progressive narrowing or widening of a piece of fabric at the edges while maintaining perfect selvedges. The shape generated depends on the number and size of the loop movements, and their frequency in relation to the loop density of the fabric involved.

Loop density of fabric is measured in terms of number of wales/unit length, and number of courses/unit length. In plain fabric a normal ratio for each is 1:1.3. However, as particular fabrics vary around that, it is usual to calculate it more accurately.

The best approach to calculating fully fashioning is to regard all shapes, including curves, as right angled triangles with a vertical dimension of the number of courses involved, and a horizontal dimension equal to the number of loops lost or gained by fashionings. The hypotenuse represents the line taken by the selvedge of the fabric.

Fig. 5.4 shows three fashioning situations represented on graph paper, the first involving a narrowing by one loop every two courses (Fig. 5.4a), the second a narrowing by one loop every course (Fig. 5.4b). The graph paper is ruled in the ratio 1:1.3 so that the angles generated are near to reality. In present day commercial practice narrowing is rarely carried out on every course. A one loop narrowing every course is translated into a two loop narrowing every two courses (Fig. 5.4c).

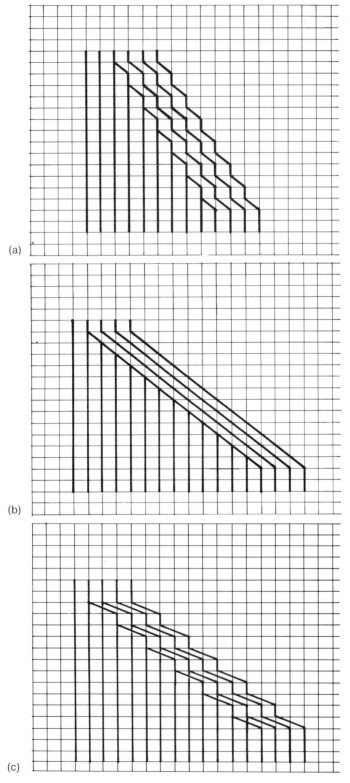

Fig. 5.4 (a) 7 fashionings × 2 courses × 1 loop (needle); (b) 12 fashionings × 1 course × 1 loop (needle); 6 fashionings × 2 courses × 2 loops (needle).

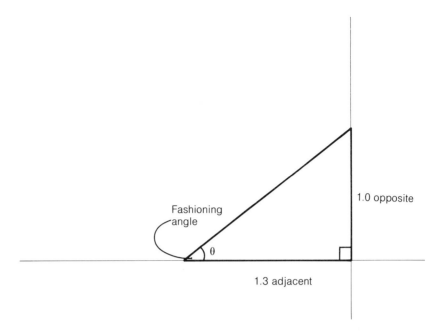

Fig. 5.5 Representation of fabric shaped by one loop every course.

The fashioning frequency of two loops every two courses is considered to be the maximum and therefore represents the lowest angle achievable by the fully fashioned process. Even at this frequency the edge of the fabric, the hypotenuse, is distorted because in reality it is formed out of the same number of courses as the vertical side of the triangle. R.W. Mills (1965) has shown that fashioning angles can be expressed mathematically, and further that the minimum angle that can be achieved is that on plain fabric produced by an effective fashioning (narrowing) of one loop every row. Apart from the practical difficulties of achieving angles below this, it must be borne in mind that the hypotenuse of the triangle formed is a distortion of the 'opposite side'. A piece of fabric narrowed by one loop every course will form at its edge a right angled triangle, the opposite side of which is in line with the wales, and the adjacent side in line with the courses (Fig. 5.5).

As the narrowing is effectively one loop every row, the adjacent side will contain the same number of wale loops as the opposite side contains course loops. As the normal ratio for courses/unit length to wales/unit length in a relaxed plain fabric is in the order of 1:1.3, the adjacent side can be given a dimension of 1.3, and the opposite a dimension of 1.

The fashioning angle can be determined trigonometrically:

$$\frac{1}{1.3} = \tan \theta$$

$0.76932 = \tan \theta$

$\theta = 37°34'$

This angle is for all practical purposes the lowest that can be achieved and sets the limitations for shape generation by fully fashioning.

The angles of other fashioning frequencies on plain fabric can be similarly calculated using the general formula:

$$\frac{\text{Fashioning frequency}}{1.3} = \tan \theta \qquad \qquad 1.$$

Example

Let fashioning frequency be one loop every four courses, then:

$$\frac{4}{1.3} = \tan \theta = 3.077$$

$\theta = 72°$

A common usage of the two loops by two course narrowing is to generate the shoulder slope on the body portions of a classic set-in sleeve garment (Fig. 5.6).

If both front and back shoulders were fashioned the resulting slope would be too great, so only the back is fashioned, the front remaining straight and terminating in a course. This throws the shoulder line seam to the back of the garment and fortuitously produces a very smooth profile.

While it is possible to work out angles from frequencies, and vice versa, most 'statements' (knitting instructions) are in fact worked out from paper patterns prepared to achieve a particular design, the fashioning frequencies being calculated directly from dimensions of the pattern and known fabric 'qualities' (wales/cm, courses/cm).

Calculating a fashioning frequency from given dimensions involves the following simple formula (Fig. 5.7):

$$F = \frac{A \times \text{w.p.cm}}{D} \qquad \qquad 1.$$

$$C = B \times \text{c.p.cm} \qquad \qquad 2.$$

A = horizontal dimension of loss of loops, in centimetres.
B = vertical dimension of loss of loops, in centimetres.
C = number of courses in B centimetres.
D = number of loops narrowed or widened by, at one fashioning.
   (Widening is inevitably by one loop only.)
F = number of fashionings.
c.p.cm = courses per centimetre.
w.p.cm = wales per centimetre.

The fashioning frequency is determined thus:

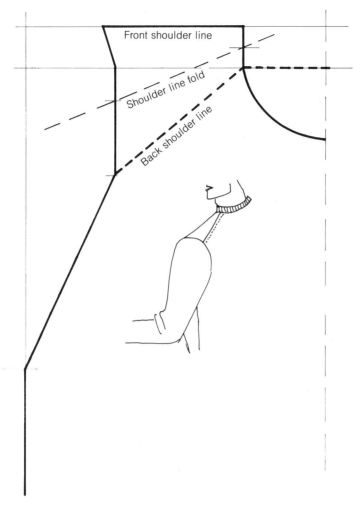

Fig. 5.6 Set in sleeve jumper showing shoulder shape construction.

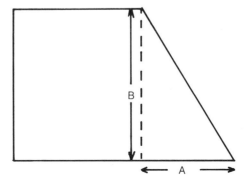

Fig. 5.7 Calculating a fashioning frequency from given dimensions.

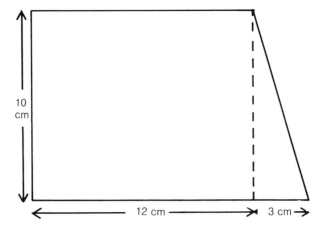

Fig. 5.8 Shaped piece of fabric: 5 wales/cm; 6 courses/cm.

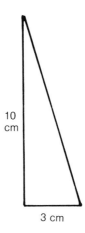

Fig. 5.9 The fashioned portion of the fabric in Fig. 5.8.

$$\text{Freq.} = \frac{C}{F} \qquad\qquad\qquad\qquad 3.$$

or

$$\text{Freq.} = \frac{C}{F + 1} \qquad\qquad\qquad\qquad 4.$$

Formula 4 allows the shaped section to begin by knitting before a fashioning, and end with knitting after a fashioning. Formula 3 is appropriate when the fashioning sequence is followed by further knitting.

Example (Fig. 5.8)

The fashioned portion of the piece of fabric in Fig. 5.8 can be represented by the triangle in Fig. 5.9;

c.p.cm = 6.
w.p.cm = 5.

Number of courses = 10×6
$= 60$

Number of fashionings $= \dfrac{3 \times 5}{1}$
$= 15$

Frequency of fashioning $= \dfrac{60}{15} = 4$

The whole of the piece of fabric can be represented by a 'statement':

Number of loops at start = $15 \times 5 = 75$
Fashioning on RH side   = 15 times at four course intervals, over one
                                                 needle space, or $15 \times 4 \times 1$
Number of loops at finish = $12 \times 5 = 60$

These simple formulae deal with whole numbers only as neither a knitted course nor a wale can be subdivided. Where C is not exactly divisible by F a remainder is created. This remainder of a number of courses can be distributed so that a proportion of the fashioning intervals are increased by one.

Example

Number of courses = 33
Number of fashionings = 6

Using formulae 3 frequency $= \dfrac{33}{6}$
$= 5$ remainder 3 courses

Distributing these remaining courses produces two differing fashioning frequencies:

- 3 fashionings @ 5 course intervals.
- 3 fashionings @ 6 course intervals.

Usually designers of fully fashioned garments avoid such situations by simplifying shapes to contain whole number frequencies.

Shapes

Commercial garments produced by the industry using straight bar knitting machinery tend to be of few types and of relatively simple shapes. This may reflect a continuing market demand for 'classical' knitwear, but there is little doubt that the full scope of shaping is not exploited in practice. There is also a built in conservatism within the fully fashioned

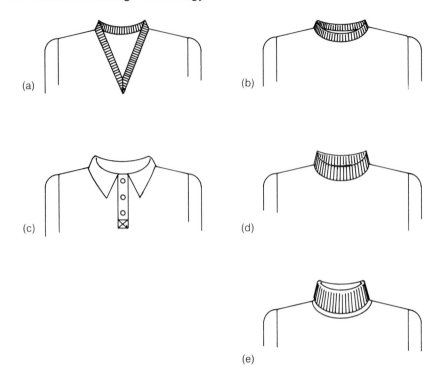

Fig. 5.10 Common knitted garment collar styles: (a) V-neck; (b) round neck; (c) shirt neck; (d) turtle neck; (e) polo neck.

industry which maintains convention fairly rigidly. Most straight bar knitting machinery is built with a limited product in mind, in contrast with V-bed knitting machinery that is built for versatility.

There are three basic upper body styles in general production: raglan sleeve, set in sleeve and saddle shoulder. Both cardigans and jumpers are produced in all three, with variations of the neck lines (Fig. 5.10) into round neck, V-neck, turtle neck, polo neck, shirt neck, and occasionally halter neck and slash neck. Both jumper and cardigan styles are produced in all the variations.

The other variable in the shape of garment produced is the treatment of waistbands and cuffs. Because of the limitation of most straight bar knitting machinery in producing fully fashioned garments in plain fabric, rib waistbands are produced on separate V-bed knitting machines. This poses a production disadvantage but is a very definite design advantage: not only can ribs of varying types of construction – 1 × 1, 2 × 2, 3 × 3, 2 × 1 etc. – be attached, but the width of rib attached, and therefore the balance of rib to body, can be varied by a device known as doubling. This is the placing of two rib loops on one transfer point at a predetermined frequency, when preparing the ribs for transfer to the straight bar machine when beginning the knitting of a panel. This has the effect of merging two rib wales into one body panel wale.

The more frequent the doubling, the more rib fabric can be used in relation to the body panel, and the less the waistband will pull in the panel. Effects can be obtained that vary from a straight up and down jacket-like effect to a very full bloused effect.

Another method of producing a waistband or cuff does not involve a rib construction at all. 'Turned welt' is the term used when the extremities of the garment waistband and/or cuff are turned back on themselves. This is done at the start of knitting the panel and involves turning back the first two or three inches of fabric and running the sinker loops of the first knitted course on to the needles of the machine so that they are incorporated into the fabric on the next course of knitting. Such a construction does not pull in the fabric in any way and is used on shirt styled garments or at the hems of fully fashioned skirts.

As already mentioned, most garments are very stereotyped in their construction. It is possible to produce garments that are unconventional but they are rarely seen in commercial production. The fully fashioned industry used to produce garments of similar complexity for underwear, shaping them to fit the contours of the body closely. Included in such garments were techniques that moved the product towards integral knitting, such as running on the wale selvedges so that the knitting changed direction, and internal fashioning.

Fully fashioning has long been used on garments other than the ones described as being the products of the present industry with its straight bar bearded needle machinery. Most other fully fashioned garments are produced on hand flat knitting machinery, either V-bed or 'domestic' single bed machines of various sorts. Classifications include:

(1) *Ladies suits, jackets and coats knitted in milano rib in fine gauges* The materials used are high quality wool yarns and mercerised cotton. Styles are very classical, appealing to the older woman, with great attention to detailing. This section of the industry is in decline.

(2) *Fully fashioned men's sweaters* It has long been most economical to produce coarse gauge men's sweaters on hand flat machines. Such sweaters range from simple raglan sleeve styles in half cardigan, to complex sweaters involving loop transfer designs or cables. Particular, specialist lines include cricketing sweaters and 'ganzies' (fishermen's sweaters).

(3) *Fashion knitwear* Since the introduction of low priced domestic knitting machines in the early 1960s, many small industries have established themselves in the production of garments of all types but with the common characteristics of high fashion content, Quick Response and small production runs. Most of the products of this industry fall into the fully fashioned category. Again this is an area where the new technology V-bed knitting machines are able to produce similar articles, and these will increasingly be available.

Modern V-bed machinery

The introduction of computer controlled V-bed knitting machinery in recent times is responsible for a widening of the range of fully-fashioned knitted garments, as well as the transfer of production of certain types of garment from traditional methods to the new technology.

Among new types of fully fashioned garments produced on this type of machinery are a full range of colour patterned and structurally patterned rib garments. Types borrowed from other production methods include Intarsia patterned garments of a complexity previously only achieved on hand flat machinery, and fair isle patterned garments only produceable by hand-knitting or on domestic knitting machines. The transfer of normal production from straight bar machinery is also taking place, particularly where the production is of garments containing expensive fibres such as cashmere. Arguments used for such transfer include quick response, little raw material tied up, short, economical runs, and capital costs not forming a major proportion of the cost of a garment.

6

Integral Garments

Right from the beginning of knitting by hand, garments were generated and constructed 'in the round'. Some of the earliest garments known are socks produced in Egypt during the Coptic era of the 4th and 5th centuries AD. These are constructed without seams, of closed loops, and display all the techniques of the integral garment. Some are very complex in the manner in which the heel pouch is generated and in the inclusion of separately knitted toes (digital socks) (Fig. 6.1).

Dorothy K. Burnham in *Textile History* analyses several socks that form part of the Walter Massey collection in the Royal Ontario Museum, Toronto. She convincingly reasons that such articles were formed using a stitching technique, i.e. single needle knitting. Because they are formed of loops they are truly knitting but do not prove the existence of the two needle hand knitting technique contemporaneously, nor do they shed light on when two needle knitting started.

Medieval caps, gloves, socks and hose were all knitted without seams and to approximate the shape of the human body, allowing for stretching of the fabric to provide exact fit where required. Later the upper body garments knitted by fishermen and their womenfolk on the northern coastlines were also produced without apparent seams.

Michael Pearson in *Traditional Knitting* repeats the advice given to him by Shetland Island knitters: 'Never ever sew when you can knit. After all most people hate stitching the knitted pieces together. Knitting in the round, together with the grafting of seams, does away with this tiresome chore'.

In terms of the techniques used in sock, glove and hat knitting, the ganzey knitters cheated. Their technique involved knitting the body of the garment in the round from the bottom up. At the yoke the knitting was either split into front and back knitting, or continued in the round to the shoulder, reserving the front neck and the underarm gusset stitches on the way. The back and front shoulders were brought together and knitted off

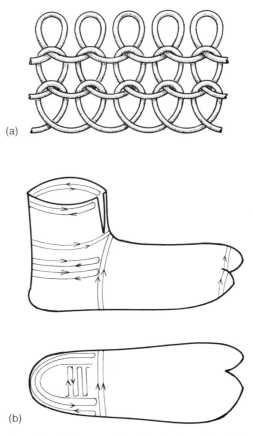

(a)

(b)

Fig. 6.1 Coptic sock, adapted from a drawing in Dorothy K Burnham's article in *Textile History* journal: (a) closed loop fabric viewed from the back; (b) right sock showing the construction, with lines representing course location and build up.

(cast off), and the sleeves were knitted by picking up the gusset stitches and walewise loops down the selvedge around the armhole.

Where the yoke is knitted in the round, the armhole apart from the gusset is cut and stitches picked up rather further in from the edge. Michael Pearson describes such a jumper as a classic Fair Isle pullover, where the extra yarn is generated and stored at the cutting line and subsequently worked into the arm join of the finished garment.

Variations of these techniques include the 'grafting' of shoulder seams, and of sleeves knitted in the round in the conventional way from cuff upwards, to the armhole of the body.

Grafting is a sewing technique in which a row, or course, of loops is generated by stitching two raw edges together. Frances Hinchcliffe describes the construction of a child's jacket in *Crafts* magazine, July/August 1982. The jacket is of 17th century English origin and has been constructed in an almost identical manner to the ganzey technique previously described, except that it has no underarm gussets and the sleeves are 'set-in' but do not have any sleeve head shaping.

Hand knitting became extremely popular towards the end of the 19th century and continued into the early 20th century. It is probably true to say that this period represented the zenith of the craft. During this period Weldon's *Practical Needlework* magazine was published. This was very influential and in its knitting series contained complete practical instructions to produce any knitted article from Smyrna rugs to knitted garters for ladies. The vast majority of the garments illustrated are integrally knitted and display all the techniques that can be used to generate shape and avoid seams and cutting.

Basic techniques

The basic techniques of integral knitting are:

(1) course shaping (flèchage);
(2) wale shaping;
(3) tubular knitting;
(4) running-on;
(5) change of stitch type;
(6) casting off.

Course shaping

In machine knitting the term flèchage (French for arrow or wedge) has been recently adopted to describe course shaping. It has also been known as the 'beret' principle of knitting. The principle is simple in that the length of the courses being knitted is diminished or extended successively. This usually takes place on one side of the knitting but can occur on either side, both sides, or indeed partial courses can be produced anywhere on the width being knitted, or the construction can occur within a tube. No loops are lost by casting off or pressing off (dropping); all loops are stored (held) to knit at a later stage. The technique in fact can be alternatively described as knitting in which wales contain differing numbers of loops. Most of the knitting contains the same number of wales throughout.

There are two alternative methods of construction (Fig. 6.2):

(1) The number of loops knitted diminishes in every row. This gives a smoother, unstepped line, but where diminution is by more than one loop small floats occur.
(2) The course diminishes every two rows. No floats occur but the construction has steps, and small holes can result when knitting on all wales is recommended.

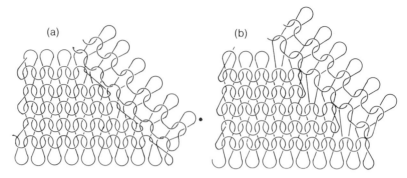

Fig. 6.2 Flèchage (course shaping): (a) number of loops diminishes in every row; (b) number of loops diminishes every two rows.

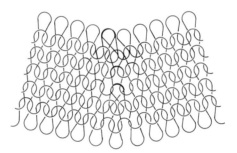

Fig. 6.3 Wale shaping.

Wale shaping

Wale shaping describes knitting in which the number of wales is reduced or increased internally within a flat piece of fabric or a tube of knitting. The number of courses essentially remains the same (Fig. 6.3).

Tubular knitting

Tubular knitting is created when the constituent thread or threads of the fabric knit spirally. Tubes are particularly useful for clothing the human body as it is made up essentially of cylinders. Tubes feature prominently in integral garments.

Running-on (picking up)

This describes the process whereby knitting is commenced on the edges of previously formed knitted fabric. Mostly the edges involved are selvedges, but one of the common uses of this technique is in fully fashioned knitted panels which are commenced on the course-wise edge of previously knitted ribs. Running-on describes the machine knitting process of placing course loops or selvedge loops on to the needles of a knitting machine. Portions of knitting can be created perpendicular to previously formed portions, or with a different number of wales from one another.

Change of stitch type

This process has already been described in cut stitch-shaped knitting. Essentially changes of fabric type between adjacent portions of a garment can generate shape. Such shapes can be horizontally, vertically or otherwise disposed to the garment.

Casting off (knitting off)

This describes the process of structure sealing the last knitted course of a piece of fabric. Up until recently this technique had been limited to hand knitting with pins or hand operated knitting machines, but the Shima Seiki company have introduced a mechanism for their model that performs this function.

Machine knitted integral garments

All the techniques discussed above are available to the machine knitter, but unfortunately not all on the same type of machinery. Some garments have traditionally been produced as essentially integral garments: half hose, hose, berets and gloves. It is only relatively recently that machinery capable of knitting upper body garments in one piece has been introduced.

William Lee's hand frame produced essentially flat fabric, and its component product, hose, was fully fashioned and seamed. However it was capable of knitting three dimensional shapes by course shaping aided by selective pressing, or by wale shaping using loop transfer techniques. It is not known whether early frames used either of these methods, although gloves and hats were produced from early times.

Berets

The traditional beret is an apparently seamless floppy hat made of wool or wool with other animal hairs. The shape varies little between sizes and different makes, the overall concept being bag-like with a close fitting head-band broadening out to a larger diameter before closing shallowly to the crown. The beret resembles in form and shape the medieval caps mentioned at the beginning of this chapter. The modern machine knitted version originated in France but has spread world-wide, being particularly popular as military headwear.

The beret shape is knitted on specialist single needle bed flat machinery, with latch needles selected by a peg drum. Above the needles are mounted sinkers to control the loops during knitting of the complex shapes.

The beret is knitted in plain fabric, its three dimensional shape formed by the consecutive knitting of up to 20 course shaped wedges. Knitting commences on the full width required and after two courses the length of course diminishes by a fixed number of loops every two courses. When only a predetermined small number of loops are being formed the cycle is repeated by knitting on the full width again. With each succeeding wedge the form of the knitting bends round through an arc, but with the head-band side restricted into a cylindrical shape.

After the last course is knitted the fabric is linked to the first course knitted. Both single chain stitch and double chain stitch are used. The blank is then milled, dyed, dried and blocked. The latter process is common in millinery and involves steaming the shape of the hat using a form. Sometimes a brushing is given to the finished form. In recent times a wide range of millinery has been produced using the beret principle combined with thermoplastic fibres. It is difficult to distinguish hats produced by three dimensional knitting from those produced by conventional means, including three dimensional weaving.

Half hose or sock

The sock is now a ubiquitous product world-wide and is worn by both sexes and all ages. Because of the nature of the production machinery the construction varies little, particularly in terms of the generation of shape. Socks very in leg length considerably, from just below the knee (true half hose) to ankle length. The small diameter circular knitting machines that produce socks impose a limitation on their structure in that it is not possible to increase the total size/number of wales of the tube of the sock. This means that there is no facility for wale shaping. The shape of the sock is created by stitch-shaping and course-shaping.

The sock is commenced at the ankle/leg opening with a welt and rib construction designed to grip the leg and prevent the collapse of the sock to a loose bundle around the ankle (often unsuccessful). Most modern socks also contain elastomeric threads in the rib to aid the grip.

After the 1×1 or 2×2 rib the structure is changed to either plain fabric or a broad rib. This section of the sock is often decorated with jacquard, semi-intarsia, wrap stripe embroidery or structural design. At the level of the heel the instep half of the knitted tube is held while knitting is continued on the heel half reciprocally. The length of the course is reduced by one loop on each side every two courses.

When the length of the course is $\frac{1}{16}$th of the circumference of the tube the process is reversed and the length of the course is increased by one loop on each side every two courses, picking up the reserved loops in the process. When the course reaches half the circumference of the tube, reciprocal knitting ceases and the spiral of the tube is recommenced.

Fig. 6.4 shows a course by course account of this process, albeit in the flat, with the structure exploded along the turning lines of the heel pouch.

After the knitting of the foot tube the toe is generated in the same

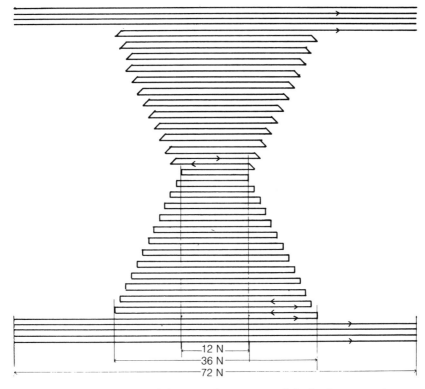

Fig. 6.4 Path of thread forming the courses of the heel construction.

manner as the heel pouch. The sock is completed by a single seam joining the two half circumferences of the tube together.

Recently the Shima Seiki flat machines of the type that make gloves have been adapted to produce half hose. The socks produced on the Shima Seiki SPF are entirely seam free and can be produced in conventional form, fully digital (five toes) or partially digital.

Upper and lower body garments

The arguments for and against integrally knitted garments were aired in Chapter 1, where it was pointed out that most of the resistance to the introduction of raw material and labour saving garment forms lay in the socio-economic objections rather than the technical.

There are technical limitations to what can be achieved; not every garment type/shape currently produced by cutting and sewing can be achieved in three dimensional knitting. But within the known possibilities only the surface has been scratched so far.

Much work has been carried out by the manufacturers of flat knitting machines into the three dimensional generation of garments. Here mention must be made of work carried out in the early 1980s by Michael

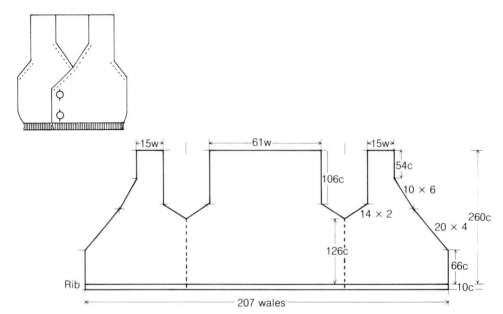

Fig. 6.5 Sleeveless jacket, design no. F035, Shima Seiki development, knitted on Shima Seiki SEC-202FF M-type. Body fabric: half cardigan, 6.6 c.p.cm, 1.9 w.p.cm. Waistband 1 × 1 rib.

Dicks, Michael O'Brien and others at the Dubied Knitting Machinery Co in Leicester, and of the work currently being undertaken by the Shima Seiki Co.

To illustrate some of these possibilities several garments are discussed here and some historical background given.

Garment 1

The first garment is an intermediate one, intermediate that is between fully fashioned and integral. It certainly saves cutting waste and reduces sewing labour but is knitted in a flat form.

The garment is a short ladies jacket knitted in a half cardigan rib construction with fronts and back knitted together and with neck revers and armholes shaped by fashioning (Fig. 6.5). The garment is a development design of the Shima Seiki Company and is produced on a seven gauge model SEC 202 FF M type. I do not propose to examine the details of the machine knitting program that achieved this article, although a brief description of the techniques involved is appropriate.

To fully fashion on a V-bed flat machine, loops are transferred selectively at the extremities of the knitting from the bed they have been knitted on to the needles on the opposite bed. The beds then move laterally to one another (racking) and the loops are transferred back, this time to different needles, either reducing or expanding the knitting width. Fig. 6.6 illustrates this figuratively.

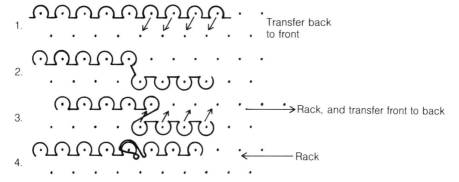

1. Transfer back to front

2.

3. Rack, and transfer front to back

4. Rack

Fig. 6.6 Fully fashioning on a V-bed flat machine.

Such movements are simple when the fabric is being knitted on one bed only but become more difficult when knitting rib constructions on both beds because there are no empty needles, other than the single ones at the outer edge of the knitting width, to which to transfer. The usual way of overcoming this problem is by knitting on only alternate needles on each bed, thus freeing needles to be used as temporary parking places for loops. This is known as half gauging. On simple fully fashioned rib garments, often only the outer three or four needles are arranged in this way, but on this garment with its internal armhole fashioning the whole knitting width is half gauged.

The only waste generated with this garment is the roving courses at the top of the shoulder portions. The only seaming required is:

(1) overlocking and taping of the shoulders;
(2) sealing of the back neck with double chain stitch;
(3) button holding and button sewing.

Further development of this garment could involve auto casting off of part or all of the shoulder and back neck on completion; and the retention of the loops of the underarm shaping while continuing to knit the front and back yokes, with subsequent knitting of sleeves. Such sleeves would require partial seaming of the head into the armhole and a top sleeve seam. Development into a raglan could eliminate the head seam. I will leave the reader to imagine the innumerable possibilities that this particular garment idea presents.

Garment 2

This garment was the invention of the late Harry Wignall, Head of the Department of Textile Technology, Leicester Polytechnic. The concept is very simple, that of knitting a tube of fabric with part way along it two opposing heel type pouches. The fabric is cut in a wale line from one end

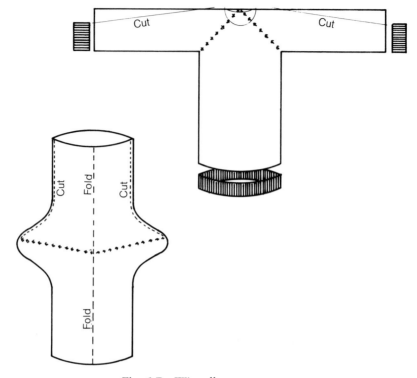

Fig. 6.7 Wignall patent garment.

of the tube to the centre of each pouch, the cut portions lowered to a position at 90° to the tube, and the basic shape of a raglan sleeved jumper is created (Fig. 6.7).

The subsequent shape requires cutting at the neck and top arm with top arm/shoulder seaming, neck finishing and rib attachments at waist and cuff. There is some saving of cutting waste with this garment but the extra seaming operations probably equal, if not exceed, those involved in a conventional cut garment of this type.

Bentley Engineering constructed a machine to this pattern and several were sold for the production of school jumpers. It is rather a dead end concept in that little if any pattern and shape development is possible; nevertheless it can be argued that this is an important link in the chain of integral garment ideas in that it uses course shaping in a very novel way, and while it shows that integral garments are possible on circular machinery it is not a versatile route.

Garment 3

This concept is one of the most promising methods of knitting integral garments on V-bed flat machines. The principle is relatively simple: tubes are knitted simultaneously for the body and sleeves of a garment. These

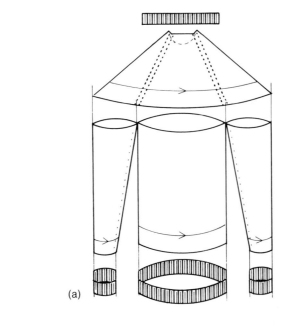

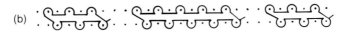

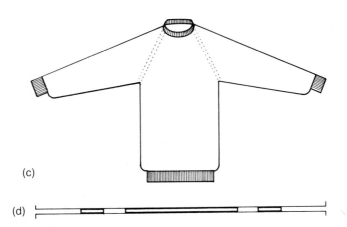

Fig. 6.8 Tubular garment: (a) breakdown of garment components; (b) loop diagram of tubes; (c) finished garment; (d) disposition of garment parts on V-bed flat knitting machine.

are spaced appropriately on the needle bed: sleeve–body–sleeve (Fig. 6.8). Between each sleeve and the body is a precise number of needles. As the knitting of the body and sleeves progresses these needles are introduced in the sleeve sections one at a time to form the underarm widenings. Eventually the sleeves meet with the body and the knitting of three tubes is merged into one.

Narrowing now commences, involving the sections of knitting formerly associated with the sleeve tubes. The whole of the sleeve sections are moved over progressively to form a raglan sleeve head on each side of the body. Eventually the diameter of the tube diminishes to neck size. It is possible to shape the front neck during the knitting process, retaining the loops for subsequent knitting of a neck rib when the back neck has been pressed off. Such a collar requires turning in at a fold and attaching to the back neck and inside front neck with mock linking.

Waistbands and cuffs can be formed by turning welts with blind overlock or linking seams, or ribs can be overlocked or linked on. It is possible to preform ribs on the knitting machine by knitting first the front ribs on alternate needles, i.e. half gauged, then transferring loops from the back bed to the front where they are stored on say odd needles while the back rib is knitted on even needles and eventually transferred to the back bed. When both back and front ribs have been knitted, the tubular knitting is commenced.

It is not necessary to commence knitting body and sleeves at the same time; body and sleeves are rarely of the same length. It has been suggested that ribs be pre-formed and run on to the needles of machines in much the same way as ribs on to a fully fashioned machine using a point bar. While this presents manipulative difficulties with the current designs of flat machines, it would enable a wider range of rib types to be attached to the garment.

Because of the manner of fashioning by loop transference between beds, already described for Garment 1, garments of this type are essentially produced on half gauged machine set-outs. There is another machine type, however, where this is potentially unnecessary. Such machines have a loop transfer bar or bars situated above the needles, capable of lifting loops off the needles, racking, and replacing them in a changed position. The machine builders ABRIL make such a machine currently and several builders, including Stoll and Universal, have previously made such machinery. It is not known whether they actually used them for seamless garments but the potential is there for future development.

The production of tubular seamless garments was patented in the name of Robinson and Chell for Courtaulds Ltd in 1965. Courtaulds themselves did not use this idea to produce commercial garments and the patent inhibited others from developing the concept.

While the garments are basically knitted in plain fabric it is possible to decorate the fabric with a wide range of structural and colour possibilities using knitting, missing, tucking and striping as well as intarsia. The garment described has raglan sleeves but it is possible to generate a wide range of different sleeve heads of the set-in type.

While this type of garment can be made on present day machinery, it would probably be best exploited if special machinery were designed to iron out some of the problems that arise.

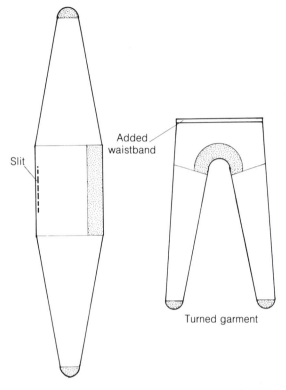

Fig. 6.9 Pretty Polly Banana type panty hose.

Panty-hose

Panty-hose have been the subject of several efforts to produce integrally knitted versions. The Pretty Polly 'Banana' type (Fig. 6.9) was an early introduction (1960s) of moderate success. The garment was knitted as a single tube from toe to toe, with the centre sections of the tube forming the panty part of the garment. A split was made in the widened panty section on one side along a single wale. This slit opened out to form the waistband but had to be finished with an elastic insertion seam. The toes were of the 'closed' variety and so required no seaming. Because of the limitations of the size of the panty section satisfactory fit could only be achieved on smaller sizes, and the idea never became fully exploited.

A more recent development by the Italian machine builder Saveo-Matec produces a whole panty hose in a novel manner (Fig. 6.10). Two open top, small diameter hose machine cylinders are mounted on the same machine frame. The upper cylinder is inverted over the lower one, in a similar configuration to a double cylinder $\frac{1}{2}$ hose machine. Both cylinders knit simultaneously, each producing one leg of the panty hose. Knitting commences at the waistband of the panty portion, each cylinder knitting· an elastomeric turned welt. The two tubes, one inside the other, are slit at the same position down a single wale, starting from the first course. On

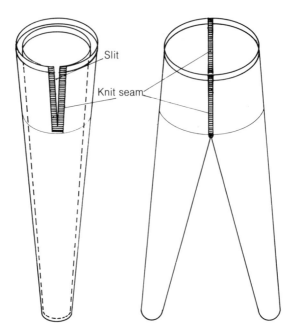

Fig. 6.10 Savio-Matec panty hose.

either side of the slit, selected needles share the yarn on some of the courses, splicing the two tubes together and forming a 'knit seam'. This splicing continues for a small number of courses after the slitting, to form the lower extremity of the seam. The legs are knitted one inside the other and have open toes that are sealed with an overlock seam as a post-knitting operation. All sizes are possible on this most unusual garment, which must be turned to draw the inner leg out of the outer.

For a much fuller account of the knitting process, and the ultra/assembler machine read Modig (1988).

7

Stitch Geometry, Seams and Seaming

The overwhelming consideration when seaming knitted fabrics is extensibility. This affects the control necessary during the seaming operation and the way in which the properties of the resultant construction are ascribed.

All known stitch types are extensible along the length of the seam. Such extensibility varies according to the stitch and seam type and the particular construction in terms of stitches per unit length, run-ins and type of seaming thread. The extensibility ranges from the minimum straightforward lockstitch seams to the maximum overlocked seams.

Knitted garments make use of the whole range of seam stretch characteristics, unlike woven fabric constructions where, with one or two exceptions, rigidity, stability and adequate strength are principal characteristics.

Some stitch types are required to cope with the unstable edges resulting from cutting knitted fabric. The component fabrics need to be gripped firmly to prevent pulling apart during wear, and the cut edges must be adequately covered to both neaten them and prevent further fraying. The overchain, or overlock, seams are used for this purpose.

Another characteristic of seams used in knitting applications, particularly knitwear, is that the threads used are often the same or similar to the constituent threads of the fabric itself. This will be dealt with more fully in examination of particular seams.

During the seaming process care must be taken to control stretching of the fabric. This is largely handled by the skill of the operative but is also aided by devices such as differential feed mechanisms on overlock machines, or the impalement on points of the linking machines and the de-skilled overlockers.

Other handling skills and devices are required to overcome the curling of plain fabric when making up in the griege state (see Glossary).

British standards

The stitches and seams described in this chapter are numbered according to the British Standard 3870, Stitches and Seams Part 1 and 2. Part 1 is the classification and terminology of stitch types. Part 2 is the classification and terminology of seam types.

The stitch types are classified into six groups, each stitch being given a three digit number. The first digit describes the class and the other two digits the particular stitch construction. The six groups are:

Class 100   Chain stitches
Class 200   Hand formed stitches
Class 300   Lockstitches
Class 400   Multi-thread chain stitches
Class 500   Overedge chain stitches
Class 600   Coverings chain stitches

In Part 2 seam constructions are divided into eight classes that describe the number and configuration of the material components in the seam.

The components are described as being limited or unlimited on their edges. Limited describes an edge that is finite and bears a relationship to the seam formed (Fig. 7.1(a)). Unlimited describes an edge or side that is indeterminate and unconnected with the seam formed. Within the British Standard a limited edge is defined with a straight line and an unlimited edge by a waved line.

The eight classes can be defined pictorially (Fig. 7.2). The complexities of different seams are illustrated in the Standard with two diagrams, one an isometric view of the components of the seam (Fig. 7.1(b)), and the other an edge view of the components accompanied by lines representing the passage of the needle(s) used to connect them (Fig. 7.1(c)).

A five digit number denotes the particular combination. The first number represents the class, the second and third digits the materials configuration, and the fourth and fifth digits the needle penetration location.

Wherever it can be used in this book the seam number will be stated. However, the lack of designation for overedge seams and for looper threads or covering threads is a serious drawback when describing seams used on knitted fabrics. There is also no convention to distinguish between stitches that penetrate particular fabric loops and ones of the same classification that do not.

Where appropriate, overedge and covering threads are drawn in the diagrams.

Single chain stitch (BS type 101)

The single chain stitch is widely used in the assembly of knitwear. It is used in seams that involve either selvedge to selvedge joins, selvedge to

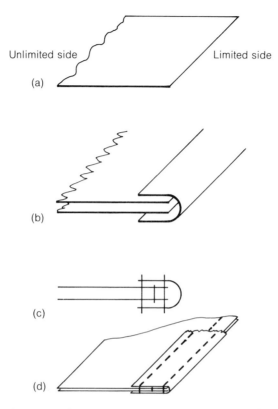

Fig. 7.1 Seam 3.13.01, BS 3870 Part 2: 1983: (a) unlimited/limited sides; (b) material configuration; (c) location of needle penetration; (d) finished seam.

centre of fabric joins, or where an edge of course loops is incorporated into a garment, as in a neck rib attachment or a course direction facing attachment.

The stitch is simple, involving one thread chained upon itself. The chain appears on one side of the fabrics joined together, and the straight advancing stitches appear on the other (Fig. 7.3). In most applications the looped side is consigned to the reverse of the seam, i.e. to the inside of the garment, and the more discreet advancing stitches appear on the outside of the garment.

The seam can be characterised by:

(1)   the stitches per unit length;
(2)   the run-in ratio of the thread;
(3)   the overall thickness and form of the particular seam construction.

The stitches per unit length, expressed as stitches per centimetre or per inch, are usually determined at the stitch formation stage either by the rate of advance of the fabric under the foot of a simple chain stitch machine, or by the spacing of points on a linking machine.

Component type	Class number							
	1	2	3	4	5	6	7	8
One side limited	2 or more	1 or more	1 or more	1 or more	0 or more	1	1	
One side limited		1 or more		plus 1 or more		— or —	— or —	
						1	1	
Both sides limited					1 or more			
Both sides unlimited	0 or more	0 or more	1 or more	0 or more	0 or more		1 or more	1 or more
minimum number of components	2 or more	2 or more	2 or more	2 or more	1 or more	1	2 or more	1 or more
basic configuration								

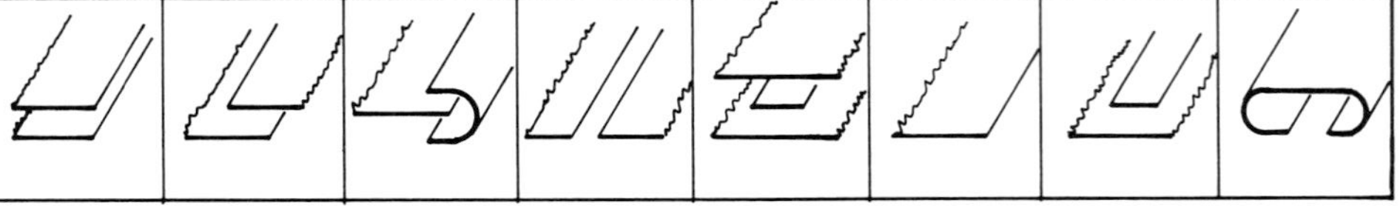

Fig. 7.2 Classification of stitched seams BS 3870.

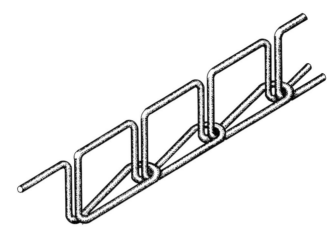

Fig. 7.3   Single chain stitch.

Run-in ratios

The run-in ratio is the most important characteristic of the seams used in joining knitted fabric. It is the ratio of the length of thread absorbed by the seam to the length of the seam.

When the run-in is relatively large, the seam is perceptibly loose and the component fabrics can be separated when pulled laterally so that the seam 'grins'. The extensibility of the seam along its length is, however, at a maximum.

At the opposite extreme, with low run-in, the seam is perceptibly tight with little lateral movement between the components and reduced stretch along the seam.

The run-in ratio in all types of seams is an absolute quantity that expresses three variables which can characterise the geometric construction of a seam:

(1)   the stitch density or frequency, i.e. number of stitches/cm;
(2)   the overall thickness of the components to be joined;
(3)   the tension of the thread at the time of construction.

These factors are best illustrated diagramatically (Fig. 7.4). In Fig. 7.4a two constructions of single chain stitch are illustrated, both with equal thickness of component fabrics. Construction 1 has twice the number of stitches/cm than construction 2, therefore the number of penetrations of the fabric by the thread is twice that of construction 2, so increasing the length of thread absorbed.

In construction 1 run-in is proportional to $3L + 16t$. In construction 2 run-in is proportional to $3L + 8t$. The fewer stitches per unit length, the less thread used in the seam (run-in). For the purpose of these diagrams the length of thread used in advancing the stitch, plus that absorbed into

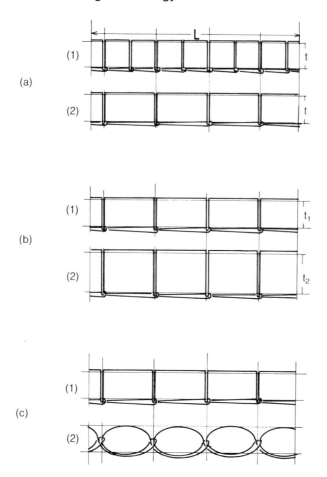

Fig. 7.4 Determinants of run-in ratios in seams: (a) stitch frequency; (b) component thickness; (c) thread tension. L = length of seam; t = thickness of fabric.

the loop of the seam, has been simplified into a quantity of three times the length of the seam.

In Fig. 7.4b construction 1 has thinner component fabrics than construction 2. The increased thickness of construction 2 absorbs more thread for a given stitch density than construction 1. In construction 1 run-in is proportional to $3L + 2t_1$. In construction 2 run-in is proportional to $3L + 2t_2$. As t_2 is greater than t_1, then, as thickness of component increases so run-in increases.

Fig. 7.4c illustrates the effect of increasing the tension of the thread during formation of the stitch. It does not attempt to show a real situation, only a trend. No absolute quantities are suggested as the geometric concepts could be quite complex. Nevertheless it can be inferred that as tension increases so the fabric compresses and the thread becomes more a series of curves, eliminating the portion of the stitch penetrating the thickness of the fabric.

Such diagrams may also serve to illustrate the dynamics of the seam being stretched along its length. The construction would increasingly move from the rectangular form to the curved form, followed by a more linear form as the seam collapsed the fabric to its maximum compression.

In the case of the single chain stitch, at the maximum extensibility of the structure the thread would still be folded into its triple formation, consisting of the two sides of the loop and the return or advancing portion of the chain. This allows a simple relationship to be formulated:

$$\text{maximum extended length of seams} = \frac{\text{run-in}}{3 \times K}$$

where K is a variable constant representing the inhibitory factors of the thickness and compressibility of the thread and fabric of a particular construction.

It is now possible to see that the three original characteristics of the seams are inter-related through the run in ratio.

Applications

One of the commonest applications of single chain stitch is in the attachment of rib collars to the necks of jumpers. Round necks, crew neckes, polo necks and V-necks can all be attached in this way. Such attachments cover a range of constructions that illustrate basic principles in the making up of knitwear. It is of considerable benefit to explore these constructions in greater depth.

The details of the composite collar constructions vary greatly but fall into three categories:

(1) *BS type 2.01.01 (Fig. 7.5a)*   A single layer of rib is overlapped with the body fabric, the raw edge of which has been previously overlocked.
(2) *BS type 3.01.01 (Fig. 7.5bi) or type 3.03.01 (Fig. 7.5bii)*   A rib collar is folded over the body fabric so that the start and finish of the rib are trapped by the stitching.
(3) *BS type 3.02.01 (Fig. 7.5c)*   A single layer of rib has a pocket of plain fabric that envelops the body fabric.

The first category of collar attachment is not common and not very satisfactory, the seam being generally too light to control the neckline adequately. It occurs on cheaper garments associated with polo necks, crew necks, and V-necks. The chain side of the stitch is placed on the inside of the garment. The collar rib itself is the outside layer and each loop on the last knitted row of the rib is entered by a chain stitch.

The second category, the folded over rib, is the commonest way of

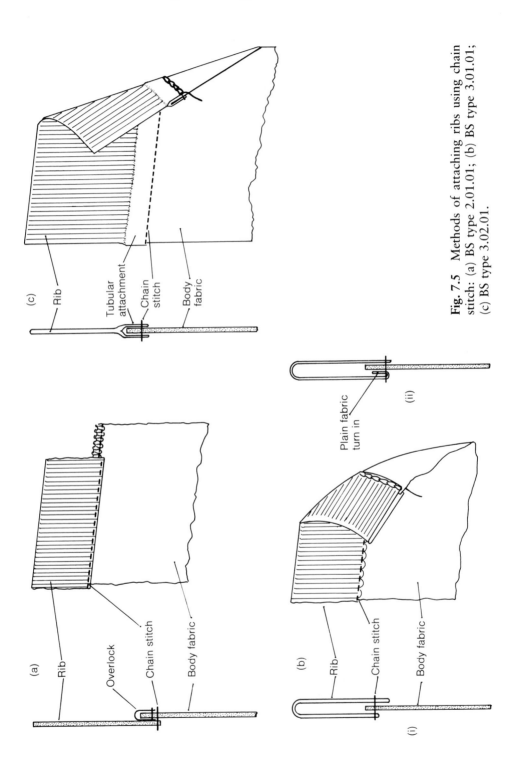

Fig. 7.5 Methods of attaching ribs using chain stitch: (a) BS type 2.01.01; (b) BS type 3.01.01; (c) BS type 3.02.01.

constructing a neck opening in knitwear. On the outside of the garment the stitches of the chain stitch penetrate the loops of the last row of rib; each individual loop is entered by one stitch in a linked seam, or randomly with at least one stitch entering each loop as in a mock linked or random linked seam. On the inside of the garment the stitches emerge just above the welt or start of the rib, and looping of the chain stitch occurs on this side.

The ribs for the collars are specially constructed and are knitted to precise widths and lengths. Each rib is knitted with a slack welt followed by the requisite number of courses, the final course being slacker to aid penetration by the linker points and needle. After the slack course a few rows of knitting provide a hand hold or roving courses to allow manipulation of the rib during seaming. After the seam is complete the roving courses are unroved, leaving the slack course trapped by the stitching.

This describes the linked version. The mock linked rib is produced in a similar way except that after the slack course the rib structure is modified into plain, and two or three courses are knitted. These plain rows curl and are often incorporated into the structure rather like BS 3.03.01 (Fig. 7.5bii). This form of rib is used on the Arndt mock linking machine.

In the third category of collar attachment the body fabric is enveloped in a pocket of tubular plain fabric developed during knitting up on the last knitted course of the rib. The rib is inverted so that it stands above the linker points, and the layers of the seam are placed on the points in order. First one side of the plain fabric envelope is run on loop for loop, then the body fabric, followed by the outer layer of the envelope. The resulting collar is very neat in appearance and is composed of a single layer of rib. All neck types (i.e. round, V, crew, polo) can be constructed using this method, but it is particularly useful and appropriate for turtle and polo neck collars where sufficient fabric is contained in the rib to fold over to the outside.

In considering the single chain stitch itself, mention has already been made of the importance of run-in and how it can be varied by adjustment of the seaming thread tension. In a typical turned over round neck collar a series of run ins were contrived that ranged from bursting tightness to visually too slack. They were found to vary from 4.5:1 to 7:1. Optimum appeared to be 6:1. Extensibility varied, with 4.5:1 having 40% recoverable extension, 7:1 having 62% extension and 6:1 having 53%. Usually 50% extensibility is required to stretch, say, a 40 cm neck seam to a 54 cm circumference head.

All the above techniques involving linking machinery can be effected on parts of garments other than neck ribs. Typical applications are cardigan and shirt facings and pocket and mock pocket details, as well as waist bands and cuffs. Increasingly mock linking techniques are used in the construction of a chain stitch seam. Such seams do not depend on the stitches entering the construction loop for loop. The frequency of stitching is such that there are rather more stitches/unit length than there

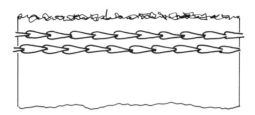

Fig. 7.6 Twin chain stitched seam.

are loops/unit length of the fabric to be joined, leading to at least one stitch entering each loop. Such constructions are often called random linking or mock linking.

Another recent introduction is the concept of twin chain stitched seams. These are formed from two single chain stitches, BS type 101, placed side by side in random linked relationship to two layers of fabric, the edges of which are cut and brushed close to the seam (Fig. 7.6). The machinery used is a modified linking machine with twin needles, cutting and brushing facility. Mathbirk Ltd make such a machine and advocate its use for shoulder seams and random linking of body portions.

One of the properties of single chain stitch is distinctly undesirable: its ability to unchain or unrove. If the thread is pulled at the end last chained, the first loop disengages allowing all the subsequent loops to disengage, a truly 'chain reaction'. If the free end of the thread is pulled through the last loop, this unroving is inhibited. Unroving can form a serious problem by reducing the durability of knitted garments.

The two thread chain stitch, see below, is much more resistant to breakdown and is often substituted for single chain stitch on all the applications of single chain stitch described.

It is quite common for a linking thread to be the same yarn that the knitted garment is constructed from. Sometimes this is used by itself or is accompanied by another thread of a stronger, more durable nature. Mono filament polyamide threads can be used, or sewing threads of cotton, cotton/polyester, polyester or modified continuous polyamide.

Two thread or double chain stitch (BS Type 401)

This stitch is more robust and more difficult to unchain than the single chain stitch. For this reason it is also known as the double locked chain stitch (Fig. 7.7). It is used in a variety of seams on a wide range of knitted garments. Often the particular application is associated with specialist machinery, such as the cup seamer used in the assembly of fully fashioned garments.

The stitch is formed from two threads, one of which penetrates the layers of fabric to be joined, while the other chains with the first thread but remains on one side only. The two threads are called the needle

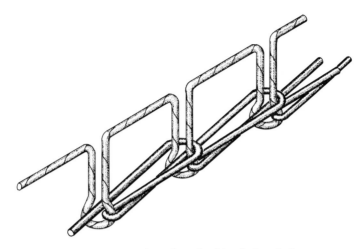

Fig. 7.7 Two thread or double chain stitch.

thread and the looper thread respectively. On the machinery that produces the stitch the threads are controlled by a needle and a looper.

The extensibility of two thread chain stitch is more limited than single chain stitch. It is complicated by the two interacting components. The needle thread, considered on its own, is constrained by its penetration of the fabrics and locking with the looper thread. If it was not so constrained it would be capable of recovering the whole of its length on extending; i.e. it would obey the general formula:

$$\text{max. extended length} = \frac{\text{run-in}}{1 \times K}$$

where K is a constant related to particular construction of fabric and thread.

However, the looper thread is more severely constrained in that it is folded back on itself so that at any point there are three portions of thread. This means that when considered by itself the looper thread can only be extended to a third of its run-in length. If the trapping involved in looping with the needle thread is absolute, the looper thread obeys the general formula:

$$\text{maximum extended length} = \frac{\text{run-in}}{3 \times K}$$

where K is a constant related to particular construction of fabric and thread.

In practice this formula more nearly represents the behaviour of the seam as a whole, although some slippage of the needle thread on to the looper side of the fabric does occur during extension. Two thread chain stitch can be used to replace a single chain stitch, although for some applications its lower extensibility either prohibits it or imposes conditions on the design and shape of that part of the garment. This particularly applies to round neck openings of the types already discussed in the section on single chain stitch.

An important application of two thread chain stitch is the cup seaming of selvedge seams of fully fashioned garments. The garment pieces are seamed in the griege state (see Glossary) and pose a problem as, being plain fabric, they are severely curled at the selvedge towards the back of the fabric. The cup seamer is designed to uncurl the fabric and control it in an uncurled state while it is being seamed.

The machine basically consists of two metal cups driven on vertical axes and mounted to form an entrapment through which the fabric is guided by hand. The two pieces of fabric are placed face to face and, after passing through an uncurling/positioning device, pass through the cups with approximately 6 mm protruding above. The needle is mounted above one of the cups so that it can pass through the protruding fabric and interact with a looper on the other side. Both needle and looper carry threads. It is important for the appearance that the seam runs down one of the edge wales without deviation. This alignment is achieved by the skill of the operative.

Three thread overlock or overchain stitch (BS 504)

Most seams applied to knitted garments of all descriptions are seams formed by three thread overlock machines. It is the universal assembly method for cut and cut stitch shaped garments. The advantages of the stitch are that it both joins and binds cut edge seams and is at the same time very extensible.

As the name implies, three threads are involved: the needle thread and two looper threads. The needle thread penetrates the fabric and is the means by which the two or more layers are joined. The loop formed by the penetrating needle thread is entered by the first looper thread, which in turn is entered by the second looper, which in turn is entered by the needle thread at the next stitch, so perpetuating a circuit (Fig. 7.8).

Several parameters of the stitch can be defined:

(1)   the number of stitches per unit length;
(2)   the distance between the edge of the fabric and the line of needle stitching (bight);
(3)   the run in of the three threads relative to the length of seam;
(4)   the balance in run in between the looper threads.

Compared to the single and double chain stitches this is a very complex construction. However, there is a limit to the number of variations possible that result in a good seam.

The 'cover' of the seam is the way the looper threads prevent the cut edges of the fabric from looking frayed and untidy after the seam has

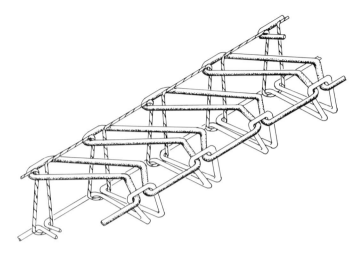

Fig. 7.8 Three thread overlock stitch.

been formed, and the extent to which they maintain that appearance. This 'cover' is dependent on two factors: the type and size of yarns used as looper threads, and the stitches per unit length.

If the stitch density is too low, little cover is provided; if it is too high the seam ripples and is hard. In fact, for any particular combination of fabric and thread, there is very little spread of stitch density that can be said to produce a satisfactory seam.

The bight of the machine is fixed and is maintained on the overlock machine itself by trimming knives that vibrate and shear off the edge of the fabric at a precise distance from the needle line. This is not adjustable because to form the stitch the loopers move through precisely prescribed arcs which differ with every bight distance.

Variable bight of a sort can be obtained on overlock machines with two needles (e.g. Rimoldi 627-00-2cd). The machine is capable of being operated with one needle only, either right or left (BS type 504), or with two needles to form stitch type 506. When operating with one needle only the two bights on the above machine are 3.3 mm and 5.5 mm, enabling a range of work from lightweight to medium weight knitwear or cut knitted fabric.

The structure of the three thread overlock seam resembles the structure of plain weft knitted fabric, with the loops of each thread forming a course, and each of the threads occupying the same general geometric configuration in relation to the other threads. When extended the structure collapses in much the same way as plain fabric, with the whole length of each thread available for the extension, restrained only by the loop interactions and the fabric involved in the seam.

The limiting factor will, in such a case, be the length of the shortest run-in, i.e. the needle thread. This leads to a proposition defining the extensions of a three thread overlock machine. The needle thread does not double back on itself and, apart from constraints from the looper threads and the fabric, is fully recoverable in length when the seam is extended i.e. the extension is proportional to the total run-in length of the needle thread.

$$\text{Maximum extended length} = \frac{L}{1\,K}$$

where L = run-in of the needle thread and K = a constant for a particular fabric construction and seaming thread.

The run-in of the threads, as already discussed with other stitches, is extremely important. Run-in of the needle thread is controlled by the same factors than influence the geometry of single chain stitch, i.e. the number of stitches per unit length, the thickness of the fabric components, and the tension applied to the thread during loop formation. These factors also affect the run-ins of the looper threads.

Variation of the tension on the needle thread, while altering the run-in for a particular construction, determines the tightness with which the components are held together. It also has a major influence on the extensibility of the seam. Variation of run-in of the looper threads affects the neatness of appearance of the seam: a high tension, low run-in results in a rippled seam edge, and a high run-in results in a general lack of control of the seam edge. Again it is true to say that the spread of run-in variations commensurate with a 'good' seam is very low.

The balance between the looper threads is also important for aesthetic and performance criteria. Imbalance in run-ins between the two looper threads results in the inter-meshing point slipping from the outer edge of the seam to a point above or below. Such imbalance leads to distortion that is both unsightly and results in deformation of the seam itself. The overall neatness of assembly of the garment suffers.

It is not the intention to describe here the detailed workings of overlock machines. However, overlock machines carry one mechanism that is important to good knitted fabric seams. This is the differential feed device – see Chapter 8.

It is increasingly common to have two needles on overlock machines. They are situated side by side 2–3 mm apart. Both needle threads interact with the looper threads to produce four thread overchain stitch (BS 506 or 512).

The four thread seam is chiefly used on heavy knitwear where the added strength and neatness of appearance confer advantages over stitch type 504. Increasingly four thread seams are being introduced to lighter constructions. An advantage claimed is that the machines equipped with two needles can be used in three ways: as a two needle overlock stitch type, 512, or by using either one of the two needles only, or to produce three thread overlock stitch 504 with two widths of bight.

The majority of three and four thread overlock seams fall into the BS 1.01 classification group although insertions of tape and elastic can be described by seam BS type 1.23.01. Hemming can be carried out with a folding attachment that allows the needle to penetrate the hem and the extreme outer edge of the folded body fabric at the same time that the edge of the hem turn is overlocked.

Seam covering or multi-thread chain stitches

The overlock seam, when used on knitted fabric, is bulky and tends to stick up perpendicular to the fabric. While this is acceptable for side seams and sleeve insertions on most knitted garments, there are certain locations on garments and certain types of garments where it is more acceptable to flatten and cover the overlocked seam with a further covering seam. Common examples include backs of neck rib seams where these are overlocked, the trimmings on the fronts of cardigans and jackets that form button stands, most swimwear seams, and some sportswear seams.

The stitch type most commonly used is the two needle multi-thread chain stitch (type 406). The needle threads occur as two lines on the outside of the garment, running on either side of the seam line. On the inside of the garment the looper thread covers and lays flat the overlock seam. Normal sewing threads are used in the needles but the looper thread is invariably similar to or the same as the threads constituting the fabric of the garment.

This stitch type (406) and its variants (602) and developments (605, 606) are also used to create seams, not merely to cover. Type 406 is used, for example, to hem swimwear, underwear and sportswear. Elastic elements can be included in such seams. A variation of this hem commonly found in men's brief construction is for a binding element to replace the hemming, incorporating an uncovered elastomeric strip. This binding can be used on both leg openings and waist bands.

Stitch type 602 is a type 406 with the addition of an upper covering thread. It is used on lapped seams when attaching trimmings such as lace edging on ladies briefs. The stitch is also used for attaching bindings and small collars to men's/boys' vests, briefs and sportswear. Complete production systems are constructed around 2, 3 and 4 needle seams of the type covering mostly BS stitch types 406, 407, 410, 602, 605 and 607. Fig. 7.9 shows a pair of mens briefs with the recommended seam and stitch types for this type of garment.

There is a strong reliance on machine attachments, each machine being set up to do a particular task. The scale of production of articles like underwear allows such specialization. It is of interest that of the four seams shown none can be designated with a BS number. As previously mentioned in this chapter, when discussing British Standards, knitted fabric seams are not well represented by the present BS/ISO classification.

The structures of the stitches described above share some common characteristics. The needle threads all produce the same simple structural configuration (Fig. 7.10), penetrating the fabric layers from one side. The

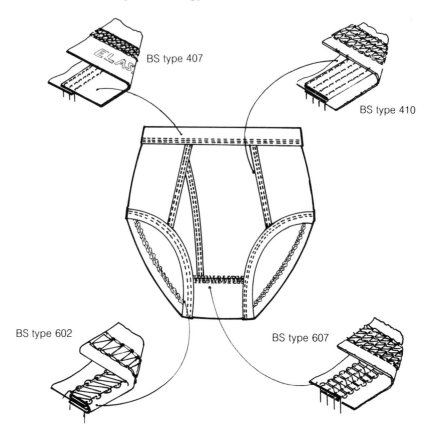

Fig. 7.9 Men's brief, assembled using multi-thread chain stitches. Reproduced by courtesy of Yamato Sewing Machines (UK) Ltd.

upper side shows the advancing stitch pattern, while on the other side the loops are penetrated by other threads or by a single thread in a looping manner, so the needle loops are connected and a 'cover' of the seam occurs.

The upper side of the seam can have a covering thread added to the structure so that cover occurs on both surfaces. The addition of an upper cover thread converts type 400 stitch types to 600 types, so that type 406 – a two needle thread and one looper thread construction – becomes type 602 with the addition of a single upper cover thread, or type 603 with the addition of two upper cover threads (Fig. 7.11).

Likewise type 407 – a three needle and one looper thread construction – becomes type 605 with the addition of one cover thread, or type 604 with two (Fig. 7.12). Type 410 – a four needle and one looper thread construction – becomes type 607 or 609 with the addition of one cover thread, or type 608 with the addition of two upper cover threads (Fig. 7.13).

Because these multi-thread constructions are relatively complex

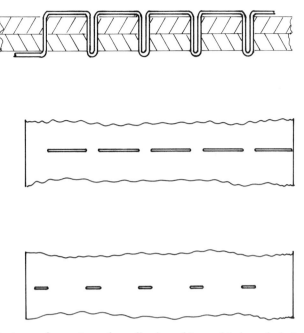

Fig. 7.10 Basic configuration of needle thread in multi-thread chain stitches.

compared to the previously described stitches used on knitted fabrics, their extensibility properties are not so readily described. They are as a class relatively stable with moderate extensibility. Because of this, within the majority of applications in which these seams are used the seam is less extensible than the base fabric, and takes the strain of longitudinal extension. It can also be said that with longitudinal stress there will be lateral compression of the seam component of such wide seams, releasing looper thread to take part in the extension.

Where greater extensibility and recovery is required elastomeric yarns are used as looper threads and sometimes as cover threads.

Lockstitch

The lockstitch (type 301) is not often used in the making up of knitted fabrics, being considered to have too low an extensibility. However, there are many occasions where woven fabrics and knitting are used in combination, e.g. woven facings on plackets of vests and shirts, woven facings on cardigans, buttons and buttonhole stands, woven epaulettes on military style jumpers, and leather trimmings and tabs and labels of all descriptions.

Lockstitch (Fig. 7.4) is the basic stitch of embroidery and appliqué work, which is increasingly of importance in knitwear and knitted

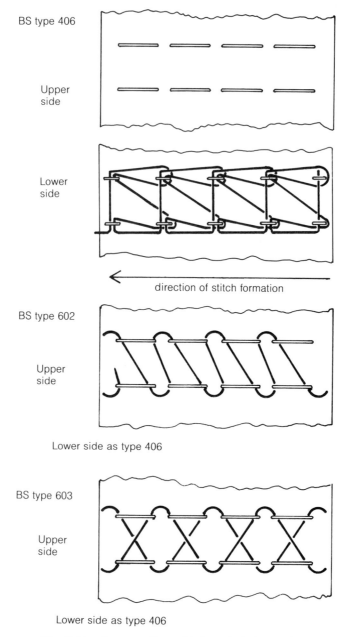

BS type 406

Upper
side

Lower
side

← direction of stitch formation →

BS type 602

Upper
side

Lower side as type 406

BS type 603

Upper
side

Lower side as type 406

Fig. 7.11 Two needle multi-thread chain stitches.

sportswear. Lockstitch appears more frequently as a joining stitch in dresses, skirts, suits and jackets made from single and double jersey fabrics.

The machinery used for the above purposes, involved with attaching relatively rigid components to knitted garments, is almost always of the

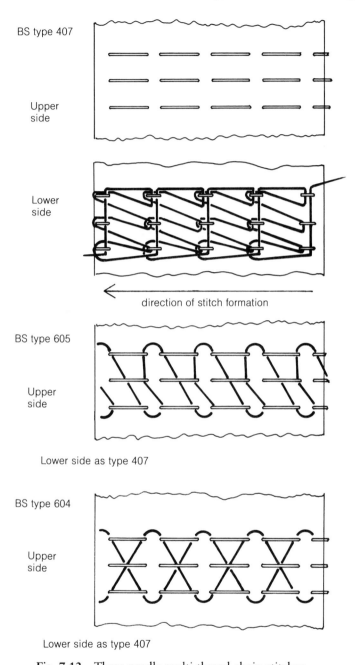

BS type 407

Upper side

Lower side

direction of stitch formation

BS type 605

Upper side

Lower side as type 407

BS type 604

Upper side

Lower side as type 407

Fig. 7.12   Three needle multi-thread chain stitches.

basic sort. The development of the machine and the use of attachments commonplace in woven outerwear manufacture are not common in knitted garment make up.

Variations commonly used in all forms of knitted garments are

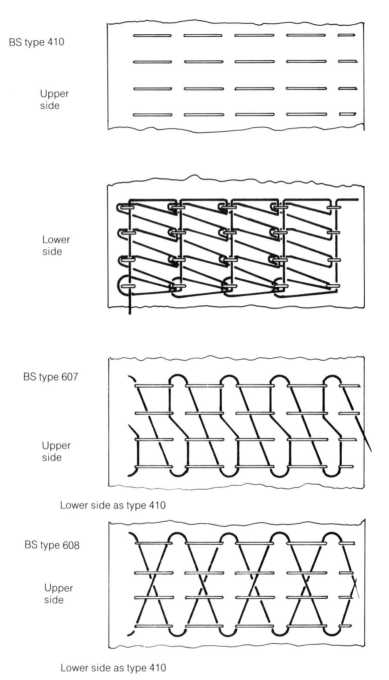

BS type 410

Upper side

Lower side

BS type 607

Upper side

Lower side as type 410

BS type 608

Upper side

Lower side as type 410

Fig. 7.13 Four needle multi-thread chain stitches.

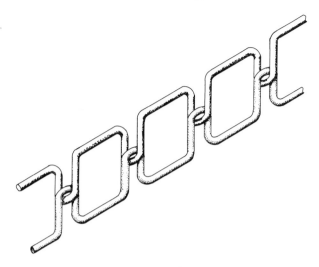

Fig. 7.14 Lockstitch.

buttonhole and button sewing, and bar tacking. The buttonhole is formed by densely zig-zagged parallel lines of lockstitching, sealed at either end with zig-zag stitching covering the two lines. A special machine is used, with a swinging needle that penetrates in a zig-zag. A special clamping foot moves the fabric in the correct way to achieve the buttonhole binding. On completion of the binding a chisel shaped knife descends, cutting the hole.

8

Machinery for Seaming Knitted Garments

Some of the machines used for making garments from knitted fabric are the same, or similar, to those used for woven fabric garment making. Others are quite specialist and are designed with knitted fabric handling in mind.

In the first category are lockstitch and chain stitch (double and single), and some overlock machines, button holers, button sewers and bartack. In the second category are linking, mock linking, cup seaming, seam covering, flatlock, and specialist overlock machinery, and it is to these that the main attention will be given in this chapter.

Most sewing machinery possesses three common constructional features:

(1) stitch forming apparatus consisting of needle(s) and ancillary mechanisms;
(2) means of supporting and presenting the work to the stitch forming zone;
(3) means of advancing the work relative to the stitch zone.

In addition to these there are usually means of adjusting the work advance to vary the stitch size or density, and means of adjusting the tension of the thread or threads. Most of the machines already mentioned have a commonality of general construction, in that the mechanism encircles the work in the form of a G clamp (Fig. 8.1). Such a construction is necessary so that the stitch forming mechanism above and below the fabric is synchronized and yet there is room for the fabric to be worked away from its edge. The overlock, or overedge, machines do not share this construction and are normally only capable of forming a stitch at the edge of the work.

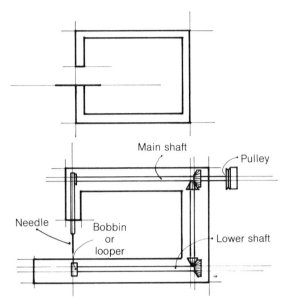

Fig. 8.1 G construction of a sewing machine.

Supporting the work

On conventional sewing machines with the G configuration, the support for the work is provided by the 'bed'. The form of the bed varies according to the type of seam, the size of the work and the location of the seam on a three dimensional garment shape.

There are four bed type variations in use in the knitted garment industries (Fig. 8.2):

(1)   flat bed;
(2)   cylinder bed;
(3)   feed off the arm bed;
(4)   overedge.

The commonest variant is the flat bed where the horizontal plate covering the bobbin, in the case of the lockstitch or the looping mechanism of the chain stitch machines, is of a plane form and is usually contiguous with and at the same level as the work top of the machine stand. Again the exception is the overlock machine where the flat bed sits above the level of the work top, which enables easy access to the loopers situated below the bed and to the front of the machine.

It is interesting that some of the new generation of overlock machines, particularly those dealing with heavy fabrics (Rimoldi type 649-00-2MF-01), are being made with the bed on the same level as the work top.

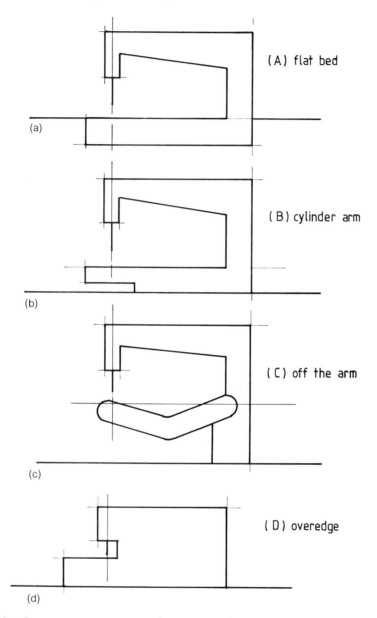

Fig. 8.2   Common constructions of sewing machines: (a) flat bed; (b) cylinder arm; (c) off the arm; (d) overedge.

The cylinder bed machines are particularly useful for dealing with already formed cylindrical shapes of garments where a lateral seam treatment or construction is required. Particular applications include hemming of the waistbands and leg openings of knitted briefs. Seam covering stitches such as Type 605 are utilised in this application with a

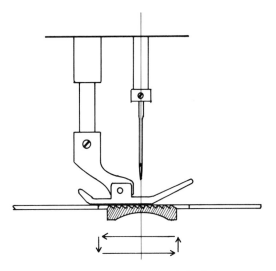

Fig. 8.3   Presser foot and feed dog.

typical machine being the Wilcox and Gibbs Type W562-32 × 356. Other applications for cylinder bed machines include the attaching of collars to round necks on knitwear and sportswear, and the blind hemming of garments of all descriptions.

The term feed off the arm beds aptly describes their function: the formation of longitudinal flat seams in tubular garment forms. Such machines are of particular significance in the manufacture of knitted garments where a seam is required to be flat for comfort and where the flat seam is formed as a covering for an existing overlock seam. The operator threads the already formed tube on the arm, or positions the two edges of an about-to-be-sealed tube on the arm, and sewing takes place, delivering the finished work off the arm.

For underwear, stitch types BS 606 or BS 607 are typically used, and for knitwear and swimwear BS 605. A typical machine of this type is the Rimoldi 183-00-4MR-04, or the Wilcox and Gibbs 41/61 series.

Advancing the work

Work is advanced and controlled during stitch formation by a variety of mechanical means and by the operative's dexterity. The commonest mechanism is the presser foot and feed dog combination, known as the drop feed. This is a feature of all the machines based on the G construction and of the overedge machines. Different means are used on the specialist cup seamers, linkers and variants.

The presser foot is a device above the work being stitched, that exerts pressure on the work to avoid it rising with the needle, to keep the layers of the work together and to maintain work contact with the feed dogs.

The pressure on the foot can be varied according to the work being stitched (Fig. 8.3).

The feed dogs are positioned below the work and perform a ratchet-like function, advancing the work one stitch forward or backward in between stitch formation. The movement is responsible also for pulling the sewing thread or threads the required amount for the formation of one stitch.

In discussing this feed dog action an understanding of the timing of a sewing machine emerges. It obeys certain principles, with the following basic steps following one another in sequence:

(1) work stationary, needle descends penetrating work;
(2) stitch formed below bed;
(3) needle withdraws fully;
(4) work advanced one stitch by feed dogs.

There are exceptions to this order which will be discussed later. The teeth of the feed dogs penetrate a polished plate that supports the work in the stitch forming zone. This plate is known as the throat plate, the throat referring to the gap through which the feed dogs protrude when in action. The feed dogs have an action common to all machine types: the dogs lift until the teeth protrude above the throat plate, the dogs move forward one stitch, lower so that the teeth are below the throat plate, and then return to starting position.

Feed dog movement can be controlled to vary the amount of forward movement; also, on some machine types, the height of the dogs can be varied to suit the particular fabrics being sewn. The mechanism is far from perfect as it relies on frictional forces, some of which are acting against the forward movement of the fabric.

The foot is exerting pressure downwards at all times, when the work is stationary or advancing. If two layers of fabric are involved in the seam, the foot is tending to retard the upper layer while the dog is advancing the lower. In spite of its drawbacks this system is very common in this simple form, especially on lockstitch machines, and has proved satisfactory with a wide range of fabrics. However, sometimes it is found convenient to use variations of the mechanism to control knitted fabrics in the stitch forming zone.

Differential drop feed

The differential feed has two feed dog groups (Fig. 8.4), one positioned in front of the point of needle penetration and one positioned after it. The front dog can be adjusted to feed faster or slower than the rear dog. In this way material can be either gathered or stretched. In lightweight fabrics this is a means of producing decorative gathering effects. In knitted fabric it is a means of overcoming the stretching induced by the

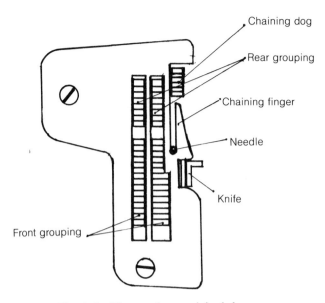

Fig. 8.4 Throat plate and feed dogs.

friction of the foot and the consequent displacement of the upper layer of fabric relative to the bottom layer.

There is a marked tendency for knitted fabrics to enter the stitching zone in a stretched condition, due both to the friction retarding effect and the compression induced by the foot. The skilled operative attempts to overcome this, but the differential feed is essential for good seaming.

On overlock machines and seam covering machines designed for knitted fabrics, typical designations for the ranges of differential feed ratios are 0.6:1 to 2:1, or 0.7:1 to 2:1, or 1:1 to 3:1. The figures show the rate of feed of the front dog to the back dog. The rate is adjusted according to the properties of the particular fabric and the nature of the particular seam.

Also of major importance in dealing with knitted fabric and the different settings is the disposition of the seam relative to the fabric, the stretch properties of knitted fabrics along the course being markedly different to those along the wale. Seams in the course-wise direction, i.e. across the fabric, are particularly difficult for the operative to control.

Other variations of fabric advancing mechanisms used when handling knitted fabric include:

(1) feeding foot;
(2) feed rollers;
(3) top feed, front and rear.

The feeding foot moves with the movement of the dogs advancing the fabric, then lifts and returns to its original position to remain static during

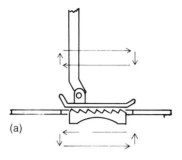

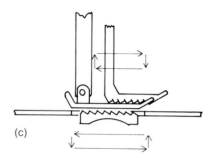

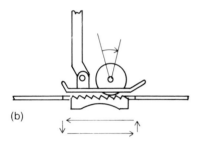

Fig. 8.5 Fabric advancing mechanisms: (a) feeding foot; (b) feeding rollers; (c) top feed.

loop formation (Fig. 8.5a). The foot can be positively driven or can merely follow the movement of the dogs on the advance and return by spring to the normal position.

Feeding rollers that are positioned behind the needle and foot are properly termed take away rollers. They are often a feature of the specialist machines designed for dealing with knitted fabrics. The device may either take the form of a single top roller positively driven against a lower extension of the throat plate, or a pair of rollers, top and bottom, both positively driven or the upper roller only driven. The rollers are intermittently synchronized with the feed dogs. Front feed rollers (Fig. 8.5b) operate before the needle, usually only on top above the dogs, and are driven intermittently and synchronously with them.

Such rollers are not to be confused with the rollers used to positively feed trimmings, bindings, and elastomeric components to the stitching zone.

Top feeds are used on some heavy duty overlock machines (Fig. 8.5c). They are similar in construction to, and replicate the movement of, the lower dogs. They are separate from the foot and are placed either in a position forward of the needle or behind it. A typical machine is the Rimoldi 647-00-2MF-20, a two needle four thread overlock machine for heavy or very extensible knitted fabrics with a front feed. Recent alterations to this machine in the Rimoldi 627-00 series involve a roller operating within the presser foot and in front of the needle.

Yamoto ZF and ZR overlock machines are fitted with a particularly well designed top feed machanism which is positively driven forward and downward. This gives very good control of the fabric while maintaining a precise gap between upper and lower dogs. The ZF machines have the top dogs before the needles; the ZR machines have the dogs after the needles.

Stitch formation

At this stage several sewing machine types will be analysed with a view to clarifying their stitch formation characteristics. For this purpose I am using, as a starting point, 'timing diagrams'. Most sewing machines perform their whole stitch formation within one rotation of the main shaft, the various motions being mostly generated by crank type mechanisms. Cranks are a means of changing circular motion into linear motion. Such linear motion is of a simple harmonic type, i.e. wave-like motion.

The various motions of the vital elements in stitch formation have been superimposed on one graph for each machine type. On the vertical axis the relative positions of the elements approximate to scale. On the horizontal axis one rotation (360°) of the main shaft is sub-divided into 20° intervals. All the timing diagrams start with the needle at its highest position at 0°.

The stitch formation is illustrated with diagrams showing the looping elements at rotational points in the cycle.

In considering sewing machines there are only two basic principles of stitch formation: lockstitching and looping.

Lockstitch

Lockstitch machinery produces stitches by the interlacing of two or more threads. In the basic stitch (BS type 301) the relationship between two threads is one of twisting. The stitches formed by this class of machinery are those described in BS 300. All the stitches are formed by a similar mechanical action in which the needle(s) penetrate the fabric either to the other side or a double penetration to the same side (needle side). On completion of the penetration, another thread (the bobbin thread) is caused to pass through the loop of thread carried by the needle(s).

This means that to effect the stitch the bobbin thread and its whole package (the bobbin) must pass through the needle loop. The bobbin must therefore be relatively small and contain a limited amount of thread requiring frequent replacement. Despite this drawback the lockstitch remains the commonest form of mechanical stitching of fabric. In knitted fabric terms, however, it is of minor importance.

The basic lockstitch machine now has a common construction pattern and loop forming system irrespective of the machine builders. Differences between machine types depend on the task it is designed to perform, with variations in robustness, speed, ability to swing needle, reverse stitch etc.

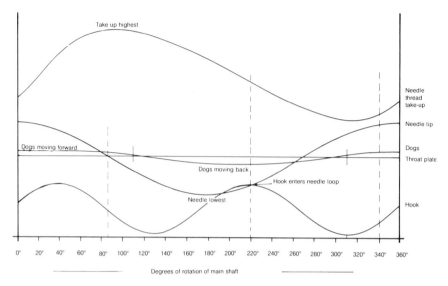

Fig. 8.6   Timing diagram for lockstitch.

The basic stitch formation can be described as follows.

Refer to the timing diagram (Fig. 8.6). At 0° the needle is at its highest point. The previous stitch has just been formed and the needle thread take up device is moving upwards pulling tight the loop formed by the needle below the work, and trapping the bobbin thread. The dogs are moving forward taking the fabric forward one stitch.

At 60° the needle is on the downward stroke and the thread take up device has pulled the previous stitch tight.

At 80° the dogs have completed the movement of the fabric forward and begin sinking below the throat plate.

At 85° the needle enters the fabric and the thread take up begins its downward movement, ensuring that there is no tautness of thread to overcome.

At 180° the needle is at its lowest, the dogs are moving back to starting position, and the bobbin hook is rotating into position to enter the needle loop.

At 220° the bobbin hook enters the slack loop formed by the needle thread as the needle rises. The needle thread take up arm is still descending, feeding slack thread to the bobbin hook as it rotationally descends and wrapping the needle loop completely around the bobbin and bobbin case.

At 270° the needle exits the throat plate and work.

At 310° the take up arm reaches its lowest point and begins its upward movement, taking up the slack thread and beginning to pull the needle loop upwards around the bobbin case.

At 340° the bobbin hook parts with the needle thread and the needle loop is now trapping the bobbin thread.

At 360° the cycle is complete.

Three of the most important events in the cycle have been indicated by vertical dotted lines in Fig. 8.6.

The stitch forming mechanism below the throat plate consists of four parts: the bobbin, bobbin case, bobbin case holder, and hook.

The bobbin is a simple flanged thread holder with a hole through the centre. A typical bobbin holds from 50 m to 100 m of thread, dependent on its type. The bobbin loosely fits into the bobbin case, which allows the bobbin to revolve freely. The thread exits through the bobbin case, passing under an adjustable spring plate tension device.

The bobbin case is restrained by a projection to prevent it rotating with the hook. The bobbin case in turn is clipped on to the spindle of the bobbin case holder. The holder is a smooth highly polished piece of metal whose function is to guide the needle thread, picked up by the hook, both over the front of the bobbin case and behind itself. The upper part of the bobbin case holder has a nose like projection that mates with a groove cut in the throat plate.

The hook revolves on the end of the bottom shaft around the whole assembly of bobbin, bobbin case, and holder. The tip of the hook enters the loop formed as the needle is withdrawing up through the fabric. As the hook descends it spreads the needle loop around the front and back of the bobbin case assembly, aided by the shape of the bobbin case holder. As the hook ascends the loop is released and is pulled upwards by the needle thread take up arm. The speeds at which this can be performed range between 3000 and 4500 stitches per minute (spm).

During stitch formation the needle thread that passes around the bobbin case assembly moves through the needle eye during the expansion of the loop and then passes back through the needle eye, pulled by the thread take up arm. The amount of thread used to form one stitch is very small compared to the amount of thread needed to form the loop through which the bobbin assembly passes. The amount of to-ing and fro-ing is considerable. Threads used for lockstitching must be tough, smooth and of low surface friction. Needle eyes must be perfect and smooth.

Example

Passage of thread through needle to form loop $= 100\,mm$

Length of loop $= 3\,mm$

Number of times a specific location on the thread passes through needle eye $= \dfrac{100}{3} \times 2 = 66.6$ times

As the size of stitch diminishes so the frequency of passage increases.

Adjustments that can be made on these simple machines are:

(1) *Stitch size* – adjusted by altering the length of stroke forward of the dogs.

(2) *Presser foot downward pressure* – adjusted by altering the length of a compression coil spring acting on the shaft of the foot.

(3) *Thread tension* – adjusted by disc tension pressure for the needle thread and the bobbin case spring for the bobbin thread.

(4) *Height of the dogs* can also be adjusted on some machines.

Overlock machinery

The overlock or overedge group of machinery is the work horse of the assembly of knitted garments, overlock being by far the commonest stitch used in all manner of seams on all manner of garment types. The properties of the seam that make it so universal are outlined in Chapter 7. The simplest type of overlock machine is the two thread, producing stitch type BS 503. Such machines are rarely used, being largely confined to blind stitch welting on knitted underwear and jersey outerwear.

Most overlock machines are of the three thread variety using one needle and two loopers, producing stitch type BS 504. Increasingly two needle machines are employed, producing stitch types BS 512 or BS 514. By removing one needle some of these machines are capable of producing BS 504 with two differing bights.

Machines are classified according to a number of factors, including the following:

(1) *Number of needles* Single needle, two needle or three;

(2) *Needle type* The makers designation and specification;

(3) *Needle gauge* The spacing in mm between two needles or three needles;

(4) *Number of threads* 2, 3, 4, or 5

(5) *Seam type or types produced* The BS number is quoted;

(6) *Bight width* The distance between the needle and the trimmed edge of the fabric in mm;

(7) *Maximum stitch length* The maximum spacing between consecutive stitches that can be obtained by altering the stroke of the dogs, under normal adjustments.

(8) *Maximum presser foot lift* The clearance height between the bottom of the foot and the throat plate, when the presser is raised, expressed in mm.

(9) *Differential feed variation range* The range of the ratio between the movement of the front group of dogs and that of the back group of dogs, the back dogs being unity (1). If the ratio is below 1 there is an underfeed situation, where the front dogs are feeding less fabric than is being taken away. If the ratio is above 1 there is an overfeed situation or compression of the fabric, where the front dogs are feeding more than is taken away.

(10) *Dog configuration* The dogs vary in their layout considerably according to the maker and the type of work the machine is designed for. The dogs are divided into two main groupings: the

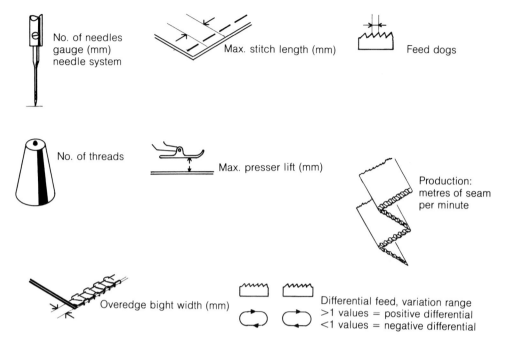

Fig. 8.7 Key to Rimoldi overlock machine specifications. Reproduced by courtesy of Rimoldi (Great Britain) Ltd.

front dogs and the rear dogs. The rear dogs consist of two sub-groups: those that act on the fabric and those that act on the chained stitch formation. The latter are called chaining dogs and their purpose is to allow the machine to chain in the absence of fabric (Fig. 8.4).

(11) *The speed of the machine* This is categorized in two ways: the maximum speed in stitches per minute or the production in metres of seam per minute at maximum stitch length.

Fig. 8.7 shows the breakdown of the Rimoldi classification and

Figs. 8.8 and 8.9 list a sample of the variants of the Rimoldi New Generation Orion 627 overlock machines built on a standard frame.

Chaining action of three thread overlock

Fig. 8.10 shows the front view of the principal stitch forming elements: needle, top or right looper, and left or lower (bottom) looper. In the diagram the needle moves up and down along the axis line shown through it. The needle is actually angled when viewed from the side.

The lower or left looper swings through an arc generated by an arm reciprocating around a lower shaft M. The dotted line L denotes the extent and path of the tip of the looper.

The movement of the upper or right looper is more complex. The

**For assembly seams
on knitwear and swimwear**

627-00 1 Needle

MACHINE									SKETCH OF SEAM	SPECIAL CHARACTERISTICS
627-00-1CD-02		3	2 (1,2) (1,5) (2,5) (3) (3,5)	3	5	0,6÷1,7		27		For very light weight fabrics. Particularly suitable for warpknit and weftknit fabrics. On request presser foot 202644-3-11 for very light warpknit fabrics.
627-00-1CD-07		3	3,3 (2,8) (3,8) (5)	3	5,5	0,8÷2		27		For light weight fabrics such as jersey, rib knit and elasticized fabrics for swimwear.
627-00-1CD-31		3	3,8	3	5	0,8÷2		27		Similar to 627-00-1CD-07 but with chaining feed dog with two rows of teeth for more efficient negative differential feed and chaining-off.
627-00-1CD-01		3	4,1 (4,6) (5) (5,6) (6)	3	5,5	0,8÷2		27	504	For medium weight fabrics such as heavy interlock, fleecy lined, terry cloth and elasticized fabrics.
627-00-1CD-06	RIM 27 -+-	3	5 (4) (6)	2,7	5,5	1÷2,5		21.6		For medium and heavy weight knitwear. With high positive differentiale feed ratio.
627-00-1CD-30		3	4,5 (3,1) (6,5)	3	4,5	0,8÷2		24		Similar to 627-00-1CD-06 but with chaining feed dog with two rows of teeth for improving chaining-off and differential feed ratio extended to negative values as well, to extend its application to woven fabrics.
627-00-1CD-20		3	4,1 (4,6) (5) (5,6) (6)	2,2	5	1÷3		18.7		For very stretchy, light and medium, soft knit fabrics. Equipped with feeding parts which increase positive differential feed action.
627-00-1MD-23		3	6 (4) (5) (7) (7,5)	3	6,5	0,8÷2		22.5		For heavy and very heavy weight knit outwear.
627-00-1MD-33		3	6,5 (3,1) (4,5)	3	6,5	0,8÷2		22.5		Similar to 627-00-1MD-23 but with chaining feed dog with two rows of teeth for more efficient negative differential feed and chaining-off.

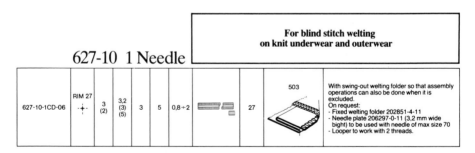

**For blind stitch welting
on knit underwear and outerwear**

627-10 1 Needle

MACHINE									SKETCH OF SEAM	SPECIAL CHARACTERISTICS
627-10-1CD-06	RIM 27 -+-	3 (2)	3,2 (3) (5)	3	5	0,8÷2		27	503	With swing-out welting folder so that assembly operations can also be done when it is excluded. On request: - Fixed welting folder 202851-4-11 - Needle plate 206297-0-11 (3,2 mm wide bight) to be used with needle of max size 70 - Looper to work with 2 threads.

Fig. 8.8   Variants of the Rimoldi New Generation Orion 627 overlock machines. Reproduced by courtesy of Rimoldi (Great Britain) Ltd.

motion is generated by the partial rotation of shaft N, lifting and lowering an arm to which a sliding piston is attached by a pivot. The piston slides through a bush that is mounted on a wheel pivoted on a fixed axle. As the piston lifts and lowers, its angular position changes. At the top of the stroke the angle inclines to the left, and at the bottom to the

**For assembly seams with insertion
of decorative piping or with insertion of reinforcing tape
for shoulder seams of knit underwear and outerwear**

627-01 1 Needle

MACHINE									SKETCH OF SEAM	SPECIAL CHARACTERISTICS
627-01-1CD-09		3	3,8	3	5	0,8÷2		27	504	For assembly seaming with insertion of a tape with raised outline or of a U-folded knit strip (with or without piping cord) between the two fabrics edges. Particularly suitable for assembly seams on shoulders, raglan sleeves, yoke and trouser sides of track suits, pyjamas and sportswear.
627-01-1CD-04	RIM 27	3	3,3 (2,8) (3,8) (5)	3	5,5	0,8÷2		27		For inserting a reinforcing tape on light weight knitwear. Tape up to 8 mm (5/16") wide.
627-01-1CD-05		3	3,8	3	5	0,8÷2		27		Similar to 627-01-1CD-04 but with chaining feed dog with two rows of teeth for more efficient negative differential feed and chaining-off.
627-01-1CD-02		3	4,1 (4,6) (5) (5,6) (6)	3	5,5	0,8÷2		27	504	For inserting a reinforcing tape on medium weight knitwear. Tape up to 8 mm (5/16") wide.
627-01-1CD-03		3	5 (4) (6)	2,7	5,5	1÷2,5		21.6		For inserting a reinforcing tape on medium and heavy weight knitwear. Tape up to 12 mm (15/32") wide.
627-01-1MD-08		3	6 (4) (5) (7) (7,5)	3	6	0,8÷2		22.5		For inserting a reinforcing tape on heavy and very heavy weight knitwear. Tape up to 12 mm (15/32") wide.

**For assemby seams with insertion
of reinforcing tape for shoulder seams
of poullover, cardigan, etc.**

627-01 2 Needles

MACHINE								SKETCH OF SEAM	SPECIAL CHARACTERISTICS
627-01-2CD-05	RIM 27 / 2,5	4	7 (5,5) (8)	3	5	0,8÷2	24	512	For medium and heavy weight knit outerwear. Tape up to 12 mm wide.
627-01-2CD-06	RIM 26 / 2	4	5,5 (4) (6,5) (7,5)	3	5	0,8÷2	24		Similar to 627-01-2CD-05 but with 2 mm needle gauge.
627-01-2MD-07	RIM 27 / 2,5	4	7 (5,5) (7,5)	3	6,5	0,8÷2	21	514	For heavy and very heavy weight knit outerwear. Tape up to 12 mm (15/32")) wide.
627-01-2MD-11	5,5 (4) (6,5) (7,5) / RIM 26	4		3	6,5	0,8÷2	22.5		Similar to 627-01-2MD-07 but wih 2 mm needle gauge.
627-01-2CD-20	/ 2	4	5,5	2,2	5,5	1÷3,1	17.6	514	For reinforced seams on very stretchy, light and medium weight knit fabrics. A 5 mm wide nylon tape can be inserted between the needles. The machine is equipped with feeding parts which increase positive differential feed action.

Fig. 8.9 Variants of the Rimoldi New Generation Orion 627 overlock machines. Reproduced by courtesy of Rimoldi (Great Britain) Ltd.

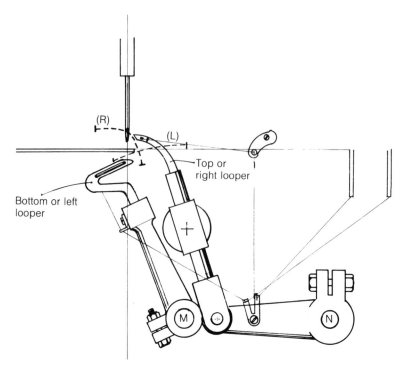

(R)

(L)

Top or
right looper

Bottom or left
looper

M

N

Fig. 8.10 Front view of stitch forming elements of three thread overlock machine.

right. The resultant motion of the looper tips is described by the dotted line R.

The path of the looper threads is shown passing through guides on the lever arm of the top looper. This acts as a take up device, pulling the newly formed stitch tight at the lowest position of the arm. Not shown on the diagram are the dogs, foot or knife.

The timing diagram (Fig. 8.11) shows the relative movements of the principal elements during a cycle of the main shaft forming one stitch. The cycle begins at 0° with the needle at its highest point. The needle movement is relative to the horizontal line showing the position of the throat plate. In particular this shows that the dogs move forward when the needle is withdrawn from the fabric. The knives likewise cut when the fabric is static.

The lower looper is shown moving from right to left and back again, and the upper looper from its highest position to its lowest position.

The principal angular positions of the main shaft noted are at 240°, 300°, 60° and 130°; these are indicated by dotted vertical lines on the timing diagram. They correspond to the loop forming diagram shown in Fig. 8.12.

At (a) (240°) the lower looper is shown entering the needle loop formed

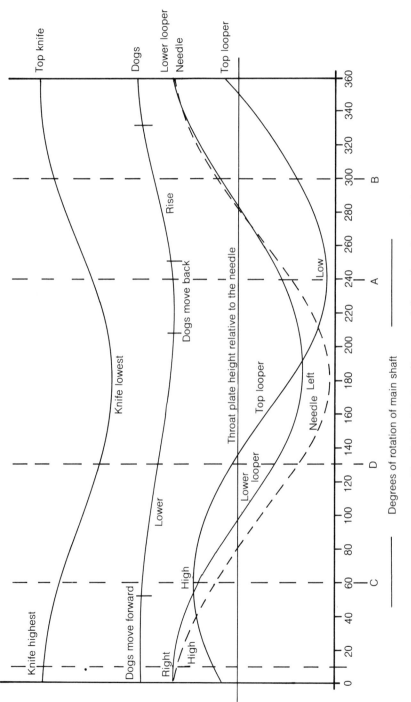

Fig. 8.11   Timing diagram of three thread overlock.

as the needle rises, slackening the thread; the upper looper is at its lowest position.

At (b) (300°) the needle has risen above the throat plate and work, leaving a loop around the lower looper. The upper looper is entering the lower looper loop on its upward rise.

At (c) (60°) the top looper is at its highest point and its loop is being entered by the descending needle. The lower loop is moving back towards the left.

At (d) (130°) the needle has descended below the throat plate and work. The lower looper is still moving to the left, casting off the previous needle loop which is then tightened by the descent of the needle trapping the lower looper loop, which is in turn cast off by the upper looper on its descent. Both looper loops are progressively tightened by the upper looper arm as it sinks to its lowest point at 240°.

Not illustrated in the loop formation diagrams is the chaining finger. This is a static extension of the throat plate (Fig. 8.4). Its function is to support the edge of the fabric in the stitch formation zone and to act as a form around which chaining takes place, whether or not fabric is present. It should also be pointed out that as the stitches completely envelop the edge of the fabric, the needle must operate in an open ended slot in the throat plate, not in a hole as in the lock stitch machines.

Also not shown in the stitch formation is the knife assembly. This operates in the zone just before the needle enters the fabric. The lower blade is fixed to the machine frame, the upper blade moves up and down once with one turn of the main shaft. The cutting action is of a scissoring nature, trimming the edge of the fabric to a precise distance from the needle. This distance is known as the bight, sometimes spelt bite. It is fixed for a particular machine and can vary between 1.2 mm and 8 mm. There is usually a relationship between the weight of fabric being seamed and the bight; for instance, a bight of 2 mm would be used on very fine gauge lightweight fabrics for lingerie and 8 mm would be used for the heaviest of knitwear.

Linking machine

Linking machines (Fig. 8.13) have a common basic construction that consists of a circular 'dial' containing grooved points that face radially outwards. It is on to these points that the fabric is placed. The diameter of the dial varies according to the particular make of the machine, and the spacing of the points varies between different gauges of the machine. The gauge is still specified in imperial measure as points per inch of circumference. For knitwear gauges are available from $3\frac{1}{2}$ points/inch to 24 points/inch.

The points remain static except in the sense that the dial revolves relative to the looping mechanism. The looping mechanism consists of two moving parts: the needle and the looper. These are carried in a supporting arm mounted internally on the dial plate, so that the looping

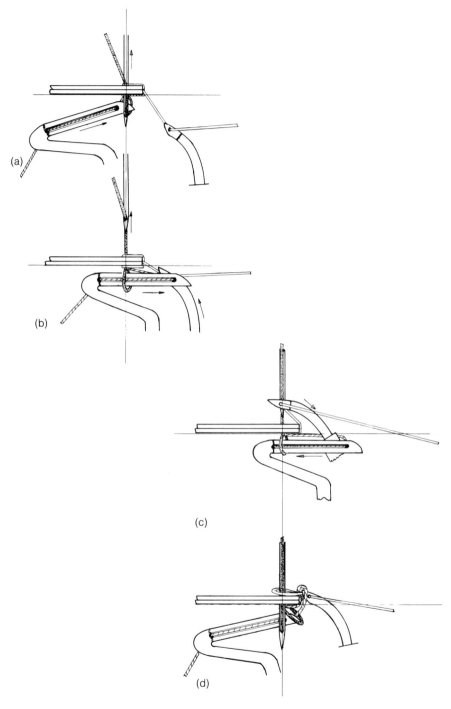

Fig. 8.12   Stitch forming action of the principal elements of the three thread overlock machine: (a) 240°; (b) 300°; (c) 60°; (d) 130°. (These relate to the vertical dotted lines on the timing diagram in Fig. 8.11.)

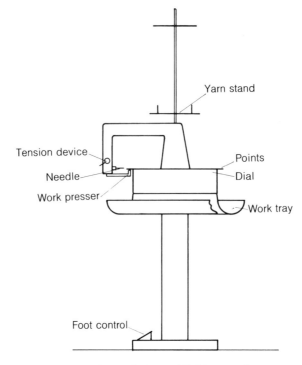

Fig. 8.13 General view of linking machine.

elements are presented in the vicinity of the points. Two variations of the machine exist, one where the needle enters the work from the inside of the dial, and the other where the needle enters the work from outside the dial and the looper works on the inside.

To complicate matters, two forms of needle exist: an eyed needle similar to those found on other seaming machines and a hooked needle similar to that used for hand crochet work. Eyed needle; the needle is usually mounted so that it enters the work from the outside, sliding along the groove of a particular point. In doing so it carries the thread with it. Once through the fabric it enters the previously formed loop held by the looper. (Fig. 8.14a).

The looper withdraws leaving the previously formed loop on the needle (Fig. 8.14b). As the needle starts to withdraw, the thread is trapped at the base of the needle, causing the loop formed on the looper side of the fabric to bell out (Fig. 8.14c). The looper now enters this loop and holds it while the needle withdraws (Fig. 8.14d). The dial now advances one point space and the whole cycle begins again (Fig. 8.14e).

The chain is formed on the side of the fabric facing the inside of the dial, i.e. on the looper side. Hooked needle; the crochet hook is usually mounted on the inside of the dial and enters the work along the groove in the point, as described before, but in the opposite direction. The thread is

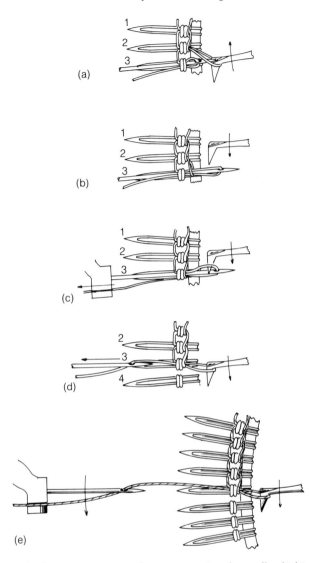

Fig. 8.14 Stitch forming action of a conventional needle linking machine forming single chain stitch.

presented to the needle by a yarn carrier. This is a tube on Complett machines, and a small ring on Mathbirk machinery. The thread enters the hook of the needle which withdraws dragging a loop through the fabric and through the previously formed loop. The needle retains the loop on its stem as the dial moves on one point and the cycle starts again.

The chaining again takes place on the inside of the dial. Both types of loop forming principles exist in reversed versions, with inside mounted conventional needles and outside mounted crochet needles.

Uses and advantages are claimed for each version. For both needle types entering from outside the dial, there is a tendency for the work to be pushed back on the points, requiring less presser plate control.

Claims are made for looping, both on the inside and outside of the dial. When looping takes place on the inside, the work is positioned with its face towards the operative, enabling the finished result to be seen. However, when placing the work on the points, in the case of turned over ribs, the vital operation of running on the last course loop for loop is carried out last and becomes more difficult because the spacing has already been determined by the running on of the more imprecise welt. In the reverse situation, i.e. looping on the outside, the loop for loop running on operation is carried out first, leading to an easier process with a result less prone to error.

Thread control is effected by two principal methods: a tension device usually of the spring loaded disc type, and a yarn take up device that controls slackness in the thread between the disc tension and the stitch forming zone.

Most linkers also have fitted a yarn trapping device that acts when the needle is withdrawing on the conventional needle type. Linkers are used in the making up of knitted outerwear in operations where a loop for loop seam is required or where a seam is precisely located down a particular wale.

Examples of loop for loop seams are closing the shoulder seams of some types of fully fashioned garments or closing the toe on socks. An example of wale seaming for precision is the attaching of a pocket to the front panel of a cardigan.

By far the commonest use of linking machines is for attaching neck ribs to knitwear (see Chapter 7). The operator of the machine sits on a seat positioned so that the dial is just below eye level. The dial and the arm are free to rotate around the central support pillar, making it easier for the operator to progress the work on to the points. Sometimes two operatives run on work to the same dial, working on opposite sides of the machine. The bulk of the garment being seamed hangs down from the points, usually into an annular cup-shaped support tray. The drive to the machine is direct and not through a clutch, a foot switch turning the motor on and off. Speed of stitching is also controlled by a foot pedal.

Cup seamer

Cup seamers have been used almost exclusively for the assembly of fully fashioned knitwear, although the author knows of machines being used for rough seaming of stitch-shaped cut panels prior to pressing and cutting.

More recently the machine has been developed by Allcock and Hashfield Ltd of Nottingham for the seaming of furs and fake furs, a use pioneered by the Rimoldi Co several years ago. The original machinery was devised and developed by the Rimoldi Company and it is one of their simpler early models that is described here. The association with Rimoldi

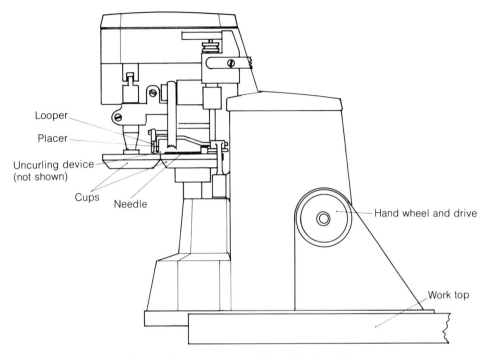

Looper
Placer
Uncurling device
(not shown)
Cups
Needle
Hand wheel and drive
Work top

Fig. 8.15   Cup seamer, Rimoldi class 155.

is so strong that world-wide this class of machinery is called the Rimoldi. A general side view of the basic machine is shown in Fig. 8.15.

The cup seamer has two 'cups' mounted on vertical axes positively driven and loaded so that a pressure is exerted at the junction where they meet. The cups act as a feeding device to drive the components being seamed through the stitching zone, and to maintain the components in a precise line of feed. A small strip of fabric protrudes above the level of the cups. It is at the base of this strip that the seam is formed. The operative contrives to maintain the height of this strip so that the seam is formed down one wale. The components hang down from the cups and are unsupported except by the hands of the operative. The looping elements, consisting of needle, looper and blind looper or placer, act in the zone immediately above the cups.

The motions of the loop-forming elements are simple and are depicted in the timing diagram and the loop formation diagrams (Fig. 8.16 and Fig. 8.17).

At 0° the needle is in its furthest back position. The needle loop is around the looper blade and the looper is at its furthest position to the right (towards the incoming work). The blind looper or placer is on the descent.

At 20° the placer throat engages with the looper thread as the looper withdraws to the left. The needle is advancing towards the work, being gripped between the two wheels.

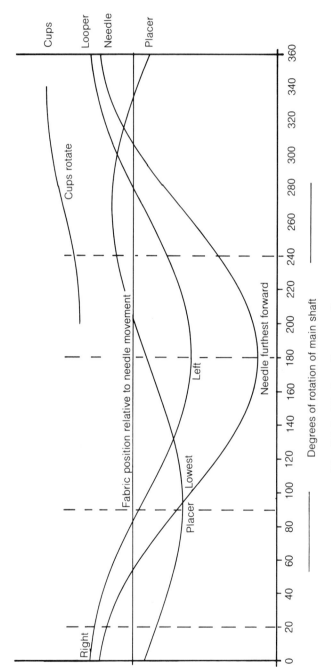

Fig. 8.16 Timing diagram of cup seamer.

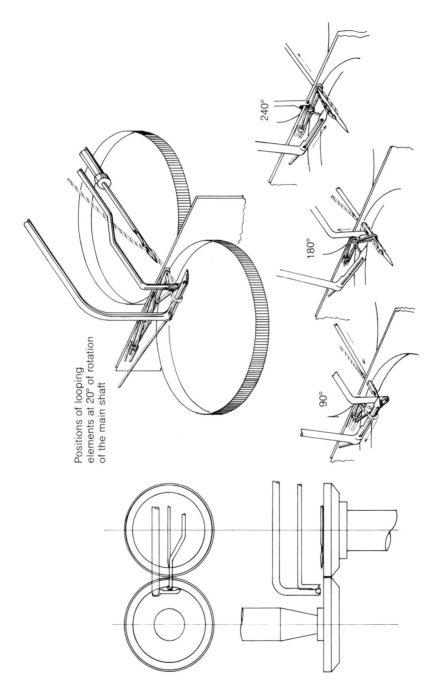

Positions of looping elements at 20° of rotation of the main shaft

90°

180°

240°

Fig. 8.17 Main working parts of cup seamer, showing stitch formation.

At 90° the placer is at its lowest, still firmly holding the looper thread and spreading it over the groove on the side of the placer. The needle tip has entered this groove above the portion of the looper loop, held by the placer. The other side of the loop is above the needle tip, under the control of the looper which is withdrawing to the left. The looper at this stage has not dropped the needle loop.

At 180° the needle is furthest forward through the fabric and the looper has swung in an arc to its furthest left and has just dropped the looper loop newly formed around the needle.

At 200° the wheels start to move forward one stitch, even though the needle is still engaged with the fabric. The looper is swinging to the right and the needle is withdrawing.

At 240° the looper tip enters the groove on the top of the needle, passing under the needle thread which is slackened due to the withdrawal of the needle. The needle continues its withdrawal and the looper progresses to the right.

At 300° the needle leaves the fabric, allowing the wheels to complete the movement forward of the fabric by one stitch. Tension is maintained on the needle thread by the movement of the needle and looper. The take up tension of the looper thread is induced by a small arm attached to the upper looper arm which has the action of lifting and drawing taut the looper loop as the looper swings to the left, i.e. between 0° and 180°.

The machinery devised and used for the selvedge seaming of fully fashioned knitwear produced in plain fabric is usually equipped with a fabric uncurling guide. This is mounted immediately before the two rollers and its function is to uncurl the rolls at the selvedge of the fabric, so that they are presented to the rings of the wheels flat. There are several versions which vary by the degree of control the operative has. The simplest type, illustrated in Fig. 8.18, is entirely hand operated, being swung into and out of action by hand and opened and closed to receive fabric by hand. The more sophisticated devices swing into and out of action via a knee press or foot pedal, opening at the same time to receive the fabric and leaving the operative with both hands free for manipulation. The height of the device can also be controlled by the operative via a knee press to adjust for fluctuating fabric edges.

The device itself consists of three plates. The centre, or fixed plate, passes between the two fabrics being uncurled. The two outer plates are spring loaded and act on the outside of the fabrics to effect the uncurling.

The uncurling itself is achieved by the peculiar shape of the plates; although it is hard to see the principle on which these are designed, in practice they work extremely well. The operative contributes considerable skill to this operation.

Another device usually fitted is a chain feed. This consists of two small nip rollers, positioned after the feed cups, that can draw the fabric away after seaming or draw the chain of stitches away if no fabric is present. The rollers are driven at the same surface speed as the cups.

The outer cup can be swivelled to open the gap between the cups,

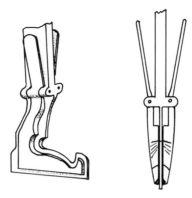

Fig. 8.18 Fabric uncurling device on cup seamer.

allowing the fabric to be positioned in between the cups at the start of the seam. Invariably the portion of fabric at the start is a rib waistband or cuff.

Developments of the cup seamer include the single chain stitch version and the two thread overlock version producing seam types BS 502 or BS 503.

Machine speeds of up to 5200 stitches per minute can be achieved but are rarely used.

Ergonomic considerations

Most of the machines described are worked by one operative from a sitting down position with the machine mounted in front of them on a stand. A stand consists of a work table, an underslung motor, a clutch mechanism and control pedals for operation by feet and knees. The vast majority of machinery is designed for right-hand working with the machine placed to the right of the work table, the drive end of the machine on the right, and the stitch forming mechanism and thus the work on the left hand side.

This arrangement enables a right-handed person to be placed slightly to the left of centre of the working zone, and to place tools, scissors, tweezers, pen and tickets on the right hand end of the work table. The right hand grips the work, feeding it into the stitching zone, and the left controls its output. On simple machines there are usually two pedals, one to engage the drive clutch, which connects the motor via a belt to the machine, and the other to operate the foot lifting mechanism. Knee operated mechanisms have already been described on the cup seamer, and attachments are also often knee operated.

Some left handed people find great difficulty in operating machinery as described, while others can adapt with lateral adjustment of foot pedals and seating position. Some left handed machines are available, a famous one being the Mauser overlock available in left and right hand variants. Shapes of machine construction have already been discussed, and these have obvious material handling implications.

Multi-thread chain stitch machines

These are also called interlock machines and seam coverers. They are not to be confused with multi-needle double chain stitch machines that employ several needles, each with an individual looper, and are particularly used in elasticating waistbands of sportswear.

The term interlock leads to confusion with the machinery that produces interlock knitted fabric. The term seam coverers only describes a limited application of these versatile machines and so is equally inapplicable.

Multi-thread chain stitch (MTCS) is used in BS 3870 and 1SO 4915 1981 to describe Class 400 stitch types. However, this simple classification is spoilt by the fact that there is a separate classification and name for the seams when an upper covering thread is added. These are called, in the standardised terminology, covering chain stitches. To compound the problem they include in the 400 series a seam with an upper covering thread, BS 408, which is in fact a two needle double chain stitch seam.

In an attempt to clarify the situation the two, three and four needle machinery that produces BS stitch types 406, 407, 410, 602, 603, 604, 605, 607, 608, and 609 will be called multi-thread chain stitch (MTCS) as they share common construction and stitch formation characteristics and are used in related circumstances to produce garments from knitted fabrics. This class of machine is widely used in the production of all types of garments made from knitted fabric, especially fully cut goods such as underwear, sportswear, leisurewear, and swimwear, but also stitch-shaped cut knitted outerwear. In the fully cut section, as outlined in Chapter 4, whole production systems can be based on these machines as they are used in a basic assembly role. They are characterized by the number of specialist attachments available to suit the machine for particular operations.

Often a particular machine is constructed with the attachments as an integrally designed part, where it is recognized that the particular production requirement is not varied over a range of garments and time. Such specialist machines include models for hemming, binding, integrating elastomeric components and attaching strappings, tapes and trimmings. Often such machines are equipped with thread cutters and trappers, tape and elastic cutters, and programmable computer control.

The use in stitch-shaped cut knitwear production is invariably limited to covering overlock seams with two needle or three needle BS 406 or 407 stitches, to flatten them. Occasionally they are used as a decorative seam exposed on the surface of the garment.

The machines are constructed in flat bed, cylinder bed and feed off the arm versions.

Typical specifications

Rimoldi 263-34-2DR-22/194-16

A flat bed machine for attaching elastic lace to ladies knit underwear, with electronic computerized device to automate the sewing and cutting cycle of the elastic.

Specification:

Two needle with top cover;
Seam type 602;
3.5 mm needle spacing;
Differential feed dogs;
Fixed trimming knives;
Elastic lace metering rollers;
Speed 5200 spm;

Fitted with 194–1C computer controller with stitch counter and photo cell inputs;
Automatic start and stop of machine;
Automatic cut of the lace at beginning or end of sewing;
Automatic presser foot lifting.

Yamato VC3645P-056L/UT-AT/AS3

A cylinder bed machine for inserting already joined elastic band into sports trousers waistbands.

Specification:

Two needle;
Seam type 406;
5.6 mm spacing;
Speed 4500 spm;

Fitted with Yamato left hand trimmer for cutting left hand raw edge of turned fabric below and at the edge of the stitch formation;
Also fitted with pneumatic thread trimmer and pneumatic folder slicer.

Machine construction and stitch formation

The needles are mounted side by side perpendicular to the direction of stitch formation. The tips of the needles are arranged at an angular displacement to one another and relative to the plane of the throat plate (Fig. 8.19). This enables the looper to enter the needle thread loops at approximately the same place in the cycle of movement, while the looper is moving from right to left and the needles are withdrawing.

The single looper is mounted on a lever arm that reciprocates,

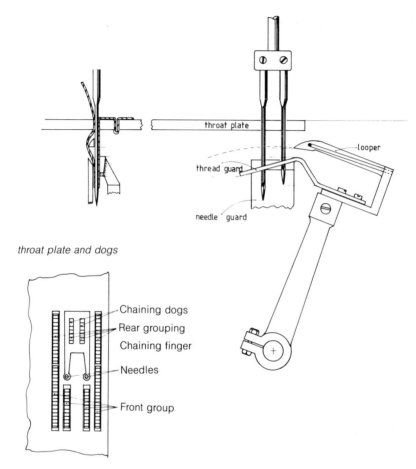

throat plate and dogs

Chaining dogs
Rear grouping
Chaining finger
Needles
Front group

Fig. 8.19 (a) Principal stitch forming parts of two needle multi-thread chain stitch; (b) throat plate and dogs.

generating an arc-like motion. The looper swings in this arc below the throat plate.

The timing diagram (Fig. 8.20) shows the relative movements of the looper, needles and dogs for a two needle machine. The needle movement is drawn to scale and is shown relative to the upper surface of the throat plate. The loopers movement, being at right angles to the needles, is shown to scale in relation to the central axes of the two needles. The vertical lines indicate the significant events in the cycle of stitch formation, and relate to the staged diagrams in Fig. 8.21.

At 0° the needles are at their highest and the looper is at its furthest left, still engaging the previously entered needle loops. Before the looper starts to move right it rocks forward slightly to allow the needles to enter the looper loop behind the looper. The dogs are progressing the fabric by one stitch above the throat plate. The needle loops held by the looper are thus

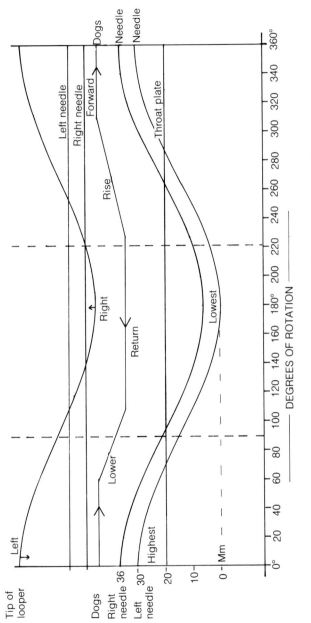

Fig. 8.20 Timing diagram of two needle multi-chain stitch.

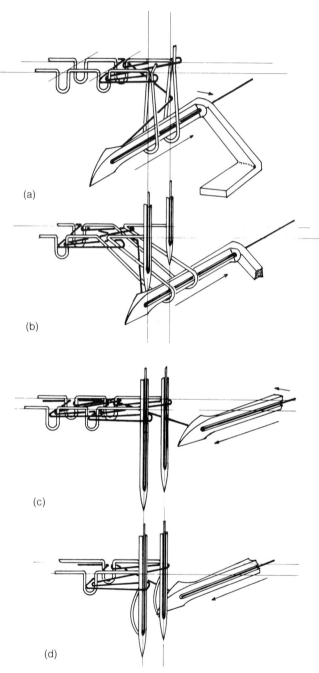

Fig. 8.21 Stitch formation of two needle multi-thread chain stitch machine: (a) 0°; (b) 90°; (c) 180°; (d) 220°.

carried forwards relative to the fabric, to the site of the next stitch. The needles lower to penetrate the fabric and the looper starts to withdraw to the right, slackening the looper thread.

At 90° the left hand needle enters the looper thread behind the looper and to the left of the previous left needle loop. A little further in the cycle the right hand needle enters the central part of the looper thread.

The looper continues to withdraw, and by 140° has dropped both previously formed needle loops. These are pulled tight by the still lowering needles, and in turn pull the looper threads with them in the reverse direction to the formation of the stitch.

At 180° the needles are at their lowest and the looper at its furthest right. The needles carry around them the previous looper thread loops. At this point the looper rocks backwards to allow it to pass behind the needles. The looper now moves to the left and the needles begin to withdraw upwards. The tension on the needle threads begins to diminish and a thread guard in front of the needles directs the slack threads to the rear of the needles so that they are entered by the looper on its return swing behind the needles. The needles are deflected forward slightly by a needle guard mounted below the arc of the looper path. The right hand needle loop is entered at 220° and the left at 250°.

The needles exit the fabric at approximately L 270° and R 290°. At 310° the dogs start moving forwards to position the needles for the next stitch.

The machine described has two needles at 6 mm spacing. It is usual to create a three needle machine by placing a further needle in the centre of the two, giving spacing of 3 mm between each. The stitch formation sequence is identical to that already described.

The dogs and the throat plate remain open between the needles to allow the looper threads to rise to the underneath of the fabric. A chaining finger between the needles allows chaining to take place in the absence of fabric.

Four needle machines share the same construction characteristics and loop forming cycle as that already described for the two and three needle machines. The upper covering thread is controlled by a spreader mounted above the needle bed and work. The spreader swings in an arc and works in conjunction with a two part thread guide.

Double chain stitch machines and de-skilled linkers

The double chain stitch (BS 401) has been described on a cup seamer earlier in this chapter. Sometimes linking machines are designed or adapted to produce it, but the version used in woven garment production with a G frame and flat bed is rarely used in the making of knitted fabric garments. It has, however, appeared as the basis of so-called de-skilled linking machines.

Popular versions of these are produced by Rimoldi, Exacta and Arndt.

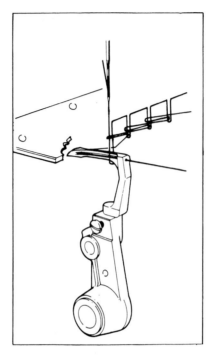

Fig. 8.22 Principal loop forming elements of the two thread or double chain stitch.

They all work on similar principles in that the work to be linked is aligned accurately so that the needle of the sewing machine enters along the knitted stitch line (usually one course) and a chain stitch is formed in at least every knitted loop of the course. To achieve this the stitches per centimetre of the chain stitch must be greater than the loops per centimetre of the knitted fabric.

The chain stitch machine has a similar loop forming mechanism to that already described in the two needle multi thread chain stitch, in which a looper enters a needle thread loop and one stitch further on the needle in turn enters the looper thread, forming a chain on the under side of the fabric (Fig. 8.22).

The Exacta Quasar 828, the Rimoldi PL 64-6000/A1, and the Arndt system all share common principles. A strip of rib is guided through a folding positioning device, so that it enters the stitching zone of the double chain stitch machine in the same form as it will appear in the garment. The garment portions are fed by a continuous belt with which they are in frictional contact. The garment portion combines with the rib immediately before the needle, the rib being wrapped around the garment position in the typical application. The yarn used in the needle is usually the same as that used to knit the garment. The machines, with very little adaptation, can be used for attaching a variety of different collar types, and also for cardigan and jacket facings.

It is arguable whether these should be called de-skilled machines as operative skill is still required although of a different order to that used by a linker. Operatives prefer using them to linking, finding that running on to points loop for loop is rather tedious. There is no doubting the productivity increase. The Quasar is quoted as completing in 20 to 50 seconds a V-neck collar that a linker would take 10 minutes to complete.

The other de-skilled machine specific to the knitwear industry is the de-skilled overlock machine. This, at first sight, seems a backward step as it involves a point dial of the same type as a linking machine. But the mechanism is simple. The fabrics to be joined are run on to the points in alignment, with the edge to be overlocked facing upwards and the garment hanging below. As the dial revolves, the fabric is trimmed by vibrating knives that ensure a bight is obtained. The fabric then passes through a stitching zone containing one needle and two loopers that together produce a three thread overlock seam. On the version by KMF a chain stitch is introduced to hold the fabrics together before overlocking takes place.

The de-skilling arises out of the perfect alignment of two pieces of fabric at a precise determined stretch on the points of dial, thus removing the overlocker's skill in feeding the fabric at the correct rate. Correct alignment of stripes in side seams is a 100% certainty, as is perfect alignment of rib cuffs and waistbands. There has been widespread introduction of this type of machine for up-market knitwear production.

9

Handling Concepts

In Western Europe attention is being given to increasing the productivity of sewing operations. During a typical seaming operation, where the work is distributed in bundle form, an efficient operative is unlikely to achieve better than 20% actual sewing time.

The time of not actually sewing is spent on a variety of tasks, including:

(1) Handling the bundle before sewing;
(2) Handling the garment, or pieces to align them prior to sewing;
(3) Handling the garment/pieces during sewing;
(4) Positioning to the needle;
(5) Handling the garment and the bundle after sewing;
(6) Completion of the ticket or other data recording;
(7) Personal time.

Added to this problem is the fact that rarely during actual sewing does the machine reach full speed. Several approaches to increasing productivity have been introduced falling under the following headings:

(1) Arranging the distribution of work to, and between, operatives more efficiently to eliminate bundle handling;
(2) Presenting the work to the operative in such a position that it diminishes handling time before and after sewing;
(3) Diminishing the data recording element or removing it;
(4) Placing attachments on to machinery to enable complex manipulation of parts to be carried out simply;
(5) Designing de-skilled machinery to replace operations that were previously highly skilled;
(6) Designing machinery with some degree of automatic handling.

Some of these approaches will be discussed in this chapter, but first it must be recognised that productivity is not the only problem that faces manufacturers in the developed world; indeed some would argue that it is not the paramount problem at all.

Makers of knitted clothing, along with others in the fashion industry, are faced with the following problems that affect the way in which production is organised:

(1) *Quick Response*   Increasingly retail and wholesale customers want garments 'tomorrow'.
(2) *Reducing work in progress*   This is allied to Quick Response, but a long time in the production process represents expensive money tied up and not being turned over.
(3) *Radically reduced order sizes*   Retailers are offering greater choice of designs/styles and do not wish to hold stock.
(4) *Assured Quality*   Any increase in productivity can be rapidly over-taken by a reduction in the quality of the output. Increasingly both the intermediate customer and the consumer are demanding quality assurance and are willing to return unsatisfactory garments that contain induced as well as designed faults.
(5) *The need to attract and keep trained workers*   This is arguably the most important factor of all. The sewing trades have never enjoyed respectability and attracting workers with the right aptitudes presents many firms with a major headache.

It is important at this stage to examine in general terms the way in which the work is organised, and look at new approaches to addressing the challenges posed by the above factors.

Traditional production systems

Traditional production systems, prevalent in both woven and knitted clothing manufacture, are often called bundle systems. The name arises because the characteristic progressing of work is in the form of a bundle containing the majority of the components to make a variable quantity of garments. The quantity varies according to the size/weight of the garment being produced. The bundle is untied at each work station, the task completed by the operative, the appropriate mark made on the production ticket, or a segment detached and the bundle re-tied to be passed on.

It is arguable that the bundle is the least important characteristic of this system. I prefer the term 'production line'.

The production line is characterized as follows:

(1) machines and operatives arranged in linear series approximating to the normal flow of work, or order of make-up;
(2) operatives confined to a single work station with work transported to them in bundle form;
(3) the operation at each work station broken down into a simple task requiring minimal skill;

(4) supervisors responsible for the flow of work between operatives and for reaction to problems such as bottlenecks;
(5) managers responsible for the overall planning of the passage of orders and batches through the system;
(6) operatives, while being held responsible for the 'quality' of their work, having little control over the nature of the task set for them;
(7) payment of the operatives by piece-rate.

Such systems arose because since the second world war garment production has been largely viewed as a mass production process. This is product dominated and price led. Such views are not held throughout the developed world, but have persisted in the UK and the USA, although for different reasons.

In the USA the sheer size of the market for any particular article has led to the dominance of mass production systems in most manufactured articles including the whole range of knitted products. In the UK the pressure has come from the dominance of a few large retail outlets with powerful purchasing power. Their sourcing policies have led to medium to large orders of low value garments with low profitability.

However, the 'market' revolution of the 1980s in the UK and elsewhere with the intrusion of small design/market led companies into retail operations, had led to smaller orders, quality assurance, less pressure on price and profitability and a movement to offshore production of articles like men's underwear.

The large chain stores and mail order companies have themselves reduced their batch/order sizes dramatically and have become more design conscious. In this context a large order for a particular type of garment is between 5000 and 10 000 dozen garments (60 000 to 120 000 garments), smaller orders/batches are any size between three dozen and 3000 dozen.

The production line is not suited to small orders, largely because piecework encourages low flexibility, with operatives preferring long runs of a particular operation. A different operation immediately lowers an operative's piece-rate income while she/he learns the new skills required. Compensatory payments during the learning process do not on the whole adequately compensate the operative for what they see as a disruption.

For a similar reason operatives perceive being multiskilled as a distinct disadvantage, being more likely to be moved round the production line to the disadvantage of their earnings. The operatives then see their role as maintaining output at all costs to optimize their earnings at the expense of quality and personal job satisfaction.

Management sees its role also as price-driven, with pressure to drive down the standard minutes for a job. The stance towards the operatives is therefore largely confrontational and could be characterized as authoritarian.

Farrands and Totterdil summarise the operatives' view of their jobs as follows:

- lack of self esteem as skilled workers;
- perception of the industry as unstable and not able to offer security;
- management preoccupied with tightening piece-rate system and limiting earnings;
- lack of companionship and team spirit;
- quality problems throughout the production process;
- repetitive strain injuries common;
- strain and fatigue a normal factor of day-to-day working life, leading to a high incidence of accidents, illness and absenteeism;
- not a good industry to enter.

In spite of this seemingly bleak view of the industry, there are a large number of smaller firms with paternalistic attitudes towards their workforce, and where confrontation is minimal. This can be said particularly of a large number of knitwear companies. Such firms often have low operative turnover and high company loyalty in spite of the production systems they use.

Production lines have other problems beside operative dissatisfaction. Large quantities of work get tied up on the production line between operatives. The work in progress is accompanied by long throughput times, mitigating against Quick Response. Often this also means that production lines have inherent cluttered and untidy environs which can be unsafe. There are associated difficulties in locating a particular bundle/batch/order within the system. Reacting to quality problems is also extremely difficult, very much a case of only finding the problem when the order has been processed and it is too late to react. Productivity can be rapidly overtaken by a reduction in the quality of the output.

Conveyor systems

Some companies have installed overhead conveyors to solve some of these problems. In particular, conveyors are said to streamline the distribution of work between operatives and to present the work to the operative in the best possible disposition for minimal handling (Fig. 9.1). Overhead conveyors are usually teamed with a computerized production system that keeps track of work in progress and tabulates production data and wages information.

A very popular system is produced by the Eton company. It can be customized to cater for different layouts and demands of customers. The basic system consists of overhead tracks from which are suspended clamps to hold the particular type of garment. The clamps circulate around the production lines, with bypass loops to each work station.

At a work station the clamps descend to present the work at a height convenient to that particular operation. The garment usually remains attached to the clamp during sewing. Occasionally, for particular tasks, the garments are removed from the clamps either by the operative or by

Fig. 9.1 Operative at a work station of the Eton conveyor system. Reproduced by courtesy of Eton Systems Ltd.

an intermediary whose task is to rearrange them between stations. Build-ups at particular operatives can be detected and re-routing can take place. Work in progress can be diminished compared to manual bundle distribution, but this depends on the skill of the line supervisor and on how well the stations are matched to the particular task.

The system is well suited to both large production runs and small orders, but the latter require very well trained multi-skilled workers.

The conveyor system is usually associated with a computer control system with a recording terminal at each work station. The operative merely has to program for the start of each particular task he/she is allocated, and to log in and out.

There are three main claims for computer-controlled conveyor systems of the Eton 2002-30:

(1)   improved productivity of approximately 25%;

(2)   reduced work in progress;
(3)   shortened throughput time.

Additional claims are made for improved quality, reduced records handling, reduced physical stress to operatives through reduction of heavy handling, and increased job satisfaction.

It is the last point that is usually disputed by critics who argue that the traditional bundle system places operatives in close proximity to one another, encouraging conversation and group identity, whereas conveyor systems isolate workers in visually shielded enclaves. Theoretically this should lead to increased mental stress, increased absenteeism and lower quality levels. I know of no studies to prove or disprove such assertions. Other critics point out that although there is a marked drop in work in progress and throughput time it is still not good enough for really Quick Response. Eton point out in defence that the result depends on how it is used.

However, it has long been known that the traditional manual bundle handling schemes, combined with piece-rate payment schemes and the division of labour to reduce and simplify tasks also result in poor performance. Ben Johnson-Hill (1978) produces a formula for quantifying motivation when measuring productivity of sewing skills, and suggests that an M/A ratio is used to measure the productivity potential of a particular operative. His ratio accepts that different operatives have different potential:

'The M/A ratio of an operator is her degree of motivation on her operation, as measured by the comparison of her cycle time on the operation at full speed and at the required quality level, to the average time per article she achieves over the full working day.'

The ratio can be expressed as a percentage:

$$\% \text{ M/A ratio} = \frac{\text{Measured cycle time/garment} \times 100}{\text{Achieved time/garment}}$$

Humanization of work

Increasingly during the past 40 years people have been questioning the concept of division of labour started by Maudesley and exemplified by Henry Ford's production line. Such a concept is that low priced output of a product is best achieved if the stages of making that product are broken down into individual tasks that demand little skill and little training and can be performed at an accelerating rate. It is argued that the benefit to all consumers and thus society is worth the inconvenience of a few. Chaplin in his film *Modern Times* (1936) lampooned such concepts, and periodic movements attempt to turn back the clock to concepts of craftsmanship and complete individual production systems.

The title 'humanization of work' is taken from the programme of work initiated by the West German government, which is continuing under the title of Work and Technology Programme.

The Germans, along with others in Europe, have realised that society has evolved and is rejecting employment in 'industry' in favour of that in 'service industry'. Such a trend can be seen in the clothing and textile industry by the inability of firms to recruit, even in times of high unemployment.

Such pressures on society have produced various outcomes, including:

(1) the movement of people into expanding service industries;
(2) the movement of 'undesirable work' offshore;
(3) growth of 'new technology industries' (this has been very slow in Western Europe);
(4) increased automation of processes.

The Germans have been among the first to recognize that in a country whose wealth depends on the export of manufactured goods, such outcomes benefit a few but do not maintain a healthy economy. They recognized that it was important to reverse the move away from employment in manufacturing industry by making it more attractive in terms of job satisfaction and esteem, while not decreasing productivity and quality of product.

Germany is not alone in tackling this problem, neither is it the first. In Sweden the car manufacturers Volvo established production groups in the 1960s, with impressive results. The Japanese have their concepts of worker involvment in decision making and the positive building of worker esteem. The Volvo car and Japanese product quality are both evidence of the success of such approaches.

In the UK clothing industry there have been early pilot studies. The Industrial Training Research Unit (ITRU) of University College, University of London, evaluated multi-skill and group working in the 1970s. The Clothing and Allied Products Industry Training Board (CAPITB) pioneered work in 1973 with one particular company, EMCAR, with the result that this particular company has had continuous group working since that time.

A large portion of the Italian knitted clothing industry is organized into small autonomous production units that depend on small orders, rapid response and multiskilled workers.

In the UK there is currently no government-led recognition of the problem and no overall programme of research. Nottinghamshire Country Council is involved with a research programme in conjunction with Nottingham Polytechnic, Conventry Polytechnic and others, entitled Work and Technology, with an aim to maintain and improve employment in the local clothing and knitwear industries.

In the UK clothing industry several companies are pioneering schemes to make work more attractive. They are aided by the interest and initiatives of sewing machine manufacturers. The schemes have a combination of all or some of the following characteristics:

(1) multi-skill operative training;
(2) group working for complete garment assembly;
(3) individual complete assembly;
(4) hourly payment, not piece-work;
(5) high quality specialized equipment;
(6) mobility between operations, involving the operative standing during tasks;
(7) group discussions to resolve particular production and quality problems.

It has already been mentioned that sewing machine manufacturers are now heavily involved in catering for the needs of this approach. Their starting base was not, however, improving the work environment of operatives but as part of the Quick Response market demands of the 1980s. Among machine companies that offer systems of various kinds are Rimoldi, Juki, Toyota/Reece, and Pfaff/Bellow. Such systems are called modular.

Peter Atkinson of the Bellow Machine Company calls their approach 'Priority Production System', aiming to get to the customer the right products, at the right price, at the right time and in the right place. He admits that this is not the priority of manufacturers that install Bellow systems, but the following are:

(1) to reduce labour turnover;
(2) to reduce absenteeism;
(3) to improve operator and workplace environment;
(4) to increase operator interest and involvment;
(5) to increase operator responsibility.

There are a secondary set of objectives:

(1) to reduce throughput time;
(2) to reduce work in progress;
(3) to increase productivity;
(4) to respond more quickly to market needs;
(5) to improve quality.

The Bellow system is characterized by a group working in a U-shaped enclosed environment that can be regarded as territory (Fig. 9.2). The peripheries of the U are formed by the machines and connecting tables. Operatives stand or sit at the machines, which are adjustable in height (Figs. 9.3 and 9.4). A work unit for one operative may consist of more than one machine. The machines are controlled by foot pedals and their DC direct drive motors are down rated to approximately 3500 spm.

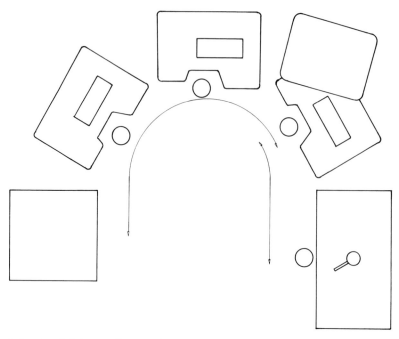

Fig. 9.2 An ACG-Ergofix standing operation layout, the basis of the Bellow modular system. Reproduced by courtesy of Bellow Machine Company Ltd.

Operatives move between stations as the need arises and are therefore multiskilled. Work may arrive at the group in bundles but garments progress as individuals. Display modules are available that indicate to the team their production success rate. Also part of the system is a sound/light paging system for calling supervisor, maintenance and other support service.

The Toyota sewing system (TSS) is very similar to the above and stresses the modular concept with two or three machines available to one operative. The individual machines are often of a programmable type. Machines can be wheeled into, out of, and to different places within the production space. Expensive, specialist machines are placed where they are accessible to several operatives.

Rimoldi produce systems specifically for knitted garment production. They offer a RIM-MOS three machine unit for the complete assembly of mini slips and swimwear. The three machines consist of:

(1) a programmable multi-operation overlock (504) machine that can in sequence produce serging seams, assembly seams and elastic insertion, with two programmable differential feed rates, two programmable stitch lengths, and elastic and chain cutters;
(2) a programmable three needle cover seamer (605) for assembly;
(3) a two needle cylinder bed cover seamer (406), for hemming with elastic insertion.

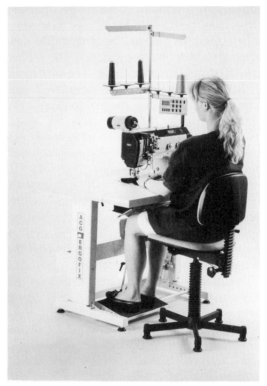

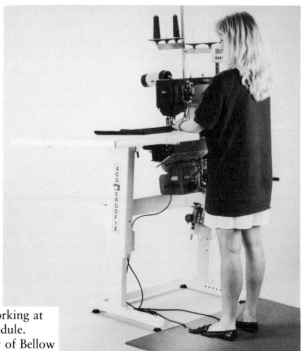

Fig. 9.3 Operatives working at machines within the module. Reproduced by courtesy of Bellow Machine Company Ltd.

Rimoldi are extending their range of sewing machines in an interesting way. Recognising that for Quick Response specific machinery may need to be assembled quickly, and that to do this with reserve machines is very expensive, they have produced their Flexsystem MO multi-operation machines and Fenix modular sectional sewing system.

The Flexsystem is multi-operational machines. One machine is programmed via computer control to carry out in sequence several operations that are normally the work of several machines. The Fenix are standard machines with a wide range of bolt-on attachments that can change the task of a three needle multithread chain stitch cylinder bed machine quickly and relatively cheaply (Fig. 9.4).

Most users of group working systems place examining and quality control functions within the group, with external sampling to check periodically that standards are being maintained. Pressing has also been introduced into group activities. Users claim that it is in the improvement of quality that the major financial benefits can lie, enabling the manufacturers to rise in the market with confidence.

The most successful schemes centre around a small team of operatives (under 10) with a similar level of output capability. Available to them is a range of assembly machines, some duplicated and some highly specialized. Machines are fitted where necessary with attachments such as hemming folders, thread under trimmers, overlock chain back latching, elastic feed etc. Some machines may be fitted with computer controls to program particular operations.

Mobility between machines is deemed essential to gain the maximum flexibility. Invariably this involves high-level standing operation. Some systems recommend two or three machines to each operative, others a ratio of eight machines to five operatives. (It is highly likely that most knitted garment applications fall into the latter category).

Machines are usually fitted with DC variable speed switchable motors that remain off until the foot pedal is depressed. This not only cuts down on wasted energy but also adds to a quieter environment. The environment is consciously kept uncluttered and some machines are fitted with pneumatic waste clearance.

Work may be delivered in varied form, from uncut fabric to sorted bundles. Work is progressed, however, in single garments and the work in progress is extremely small. Decisions about how to process a particular article are made by the group, who optimize their skills and solve production problems as they occur. A high degree of innovation often results from this approach. The team therefore is an autonomous unit responsible for its own decision making and for the delivery of its output on time and of the requisite quality.

It is found essential to pay the groups within a modular system a flat rate. Some firms also pay a production linked bonus payment. Supervisors act outside the group to ensure the group is receiving adequate supplies of raw materials and machine maintenance etc. Management, relieved of the

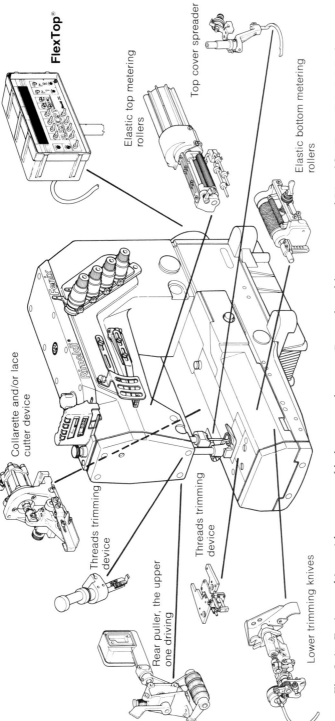

FlexTop®

Elastic top metering rollers

Top cover spreader

Elastic bottom metering rollers

Collarette and/or lace cutter device

Threads trimming device

Threads trimming device

Rear puller, the upper one driving

Lower trimming knives

Fig. 9.4 Fenix machine with a range of bolt-on attachments. Reproduced by courtesy of Rimoldi (Great Britain) Ltd.

constant confrontations with operatives concerning piece-rates, can concentrate on true production planning.

Some teams consist only of machinists, while others carry out the whole process of garment making from cutting through to final inspection, leaving only order accumulation and packing to outside the group.

Knitted garment making covers the whole spectrum, but generally speaking the cutting and initial processing of fully cut knitted garments are best done *en masse*, whereas knitwear in cut stitch shaped and fully fashioned forms suits process-right-through situations. Fully fashioned presents a unique example because assembly takes place in two stages, with a wet finishing process in between. It is only the finishing making up that is currently subject to group working in at least one UK company (Courtaulds Clothing, Worksop). One other outcome of modular or group working, noted in a number of companies, is that within the group the learning curve for new skills is considerably reduced, and training is largely handled within the group itself.

Automation

Running in some respects counter to the concepts of modular working with its craftsperson pride in product, is the 20th century obsession with automation, i.e. the elimination of human involvement in the production process.

In the clothing industries some processes are naturally suited to automatic processes and yet still allow the operative some involvement at a skilled level; the fabric spreading operation and cutting are examples. The area of making up presents challenges and difficulties to the automative engineer.

The desire to automate and de-skill arises from the already outlined difficulties of managing production lines where the operative is seen as an unreliable, expensive, troublesome source of variable quality work, in short supply and short-lived. The partial or complete removal of the operative is seen as highly desirable in this context.

Envious eyes are cast on some engineering processes where robotics and mechanical handling systems eliminate large numbers of operatives from the production of mass produced articles such as television sets or cars. The envious eyes at the same time appreciate that robotic work stations depend on the materials handled being essentially rigid, and that where flexible materials are involved local decision making is required every time a piece is picked up. Robotic systems, while capable of re-programming, are also suited to long runs of very similar articles. They are also characterized by being heavily capital intensive.

Robotics are not the only means by which automation is achieved. Making up processes are already subject to a range of techniques that essentially de-skill and shorten the time cycle of particular processes. A simple classification of such developments is:

(1) Simple machine attachments that eliminate or shorten finishing processes, such as under-bed and over-bed thread cutting and overlock back latching.

(2) Attachments to simplify what would otherwise be a difficult handling situation during seaming, such as hemming, binding and facing, folding devices, and elastomeric delivery systems.

(3) Programmable computer devices along with the associated electronic equipment, that enable sequences of operations normally controlled by the operative to be delivered in sequence and precisely. Such operations include the precise number of stitches delivered, lifting and lowering the foot, forward and backward stitching (lockstitch), introducing trimmings, cutting and trapping trimmings etc.

(4) Complete machine systems that replace other machines performing a similar task which are considered to require high skills. Included in this category are de-skilled linking systems and de-skilled three thread overlock machines for knitwear.

(5) Automatic handling devices are essentially specially built machines that carry out one specific operation. Such machines automate both the sewing machine itself and presentation and handling procedures associated with the particular operation. Clamps, tambours and velcro-surfaced belts grasp the fabric, and step motors and grip rollers propel and guide the fabric portions through the sewing zone. With the current state of technology the majority of applications are aimed at non-extensible woven fabric applications such as pocket flap production, jetted pocket insertion, and trouser and dress side seams etc.

The Japanese sewing machine company Yamato offer automatic machines for attaching elastic tape to the waist of men's briefs, various automatic machines for hemming waists and leg openings with elastic insertion for swimwear and underwear, and automatic machines for hemming with elastic insertions for the waistbands of sports trousers.

In all these applications the operative's sole role is to present the work at the start of the cycle. Robotics would of course replace the operative. Again it should be stressed that these 'automatic' systems are used on essentially mass produced garments.

All these developments have been introduced into modular working group production systems with variable success. In my view the first four stages described above are acceptable and aid the aims of group working, but automatic machines consciously reduce the operative to a robotic role that can only be sensed as demeaning.

10

Quality Control of Knitted Garments

This chapter will outline and discuss the properties and characteristics of knitted garments that are the subject of quality control procedures. The concentration will be on characteristics that are peculiar to knitted fabrics and garments made from them, as opposed to those that are characteristic of woven fabric garments. Statistical treatment and test methods are well covered in other books and publications, and will not feature strongly.

Fabric quality

The word quality is sometimes misused in knitted fabric terminology to describe the loop density of a particular fabric. There is no implied judgement of quality about this, only of quantity, i.e. number of loops in a square of prescribed dimensions: loops per square inch or loops per square centimetre etc.

This dimension – the loop density – is the most important one in defining knitted fabric properties and is directly related to appearance, weight per unit area, thickness, drape and many other factors.

The loop length (see Chapter 2) is the absolute quantity of any knitted fabric and is directly related to the loop density. In general terms, for any knitted fabric, as the loop size increases the loop density decreases. For simple fabrics the relationship can be expressed in a single equation:

$$S = \frac{K}{\ell^2}$$

where S is the loop density, ℓ is the loop length and K is a constant for the particular construction. A large amount of data and research work has been carried out relating the above expression to the characteristics of plain fabric, and definite values of K have been proposed. For other constructions, while the proposition still holds the situation is more complex and further study is required.

Course length

For some structures with complex geometry an average loop length value is largely irrelevant and expressions of 'quality' are given indirectly, either as a course length or as loop density as measured on one side of the fabric.

A course length is determined by unroving yarn from a known number of loops of the fabric and measuring its length using a crimp tester (BS Methods of Test 5441: 1977). To arrive at the loop length the mean of several course lengths is divided by the number of loops in the course extracted. It is usual to use multiples or fractions of 100 loops in this measurement.

In a circular fabric the structure is composed of a number of courses that spiral around the fabric. The number is dependent on the number of knitting sections (feeders) around the machine. Each feeder can be regarded as a separate knitting entity responsible for the course length/loop length that it is producing. Each feeder can be said to produce a different course length. It is the aim of fabric quality control to make them as near as possible to the specified value. When some courses are wildly out of specification and differ from one another, the fabric has horizontal bars that degrade its appearance and lower its perceived quality. If the mean value of the course length is out of specification, every other fabric property is also affected.

Most modern circular machines producing simple fabrics are fitted with positive feed units that ensure much closer tolerances between feeders in respect of course length. For machines that do not possess positive feed or for fabrics that cannot be knitted under positive feed conditions, a laborious setting up procedure is carried out with the machine set on producing a simple fabric, e.g. plain, 1 × 1 rib, interlock etc. The feeders are levelled using a combination of yarn speed meters and fabric analysis. When the machine is levelled to within tolerances for loop length, the necessary adjustments are made to switch it to producing the more complex fabric.

During these quality control procedures it is essential that at least one measurement is made of the work of each feeder. Modern knitting machines can have in excess of 100 feeders, so the work can be extensive.

Incoming fabric to the cutting room store would be examined for bars

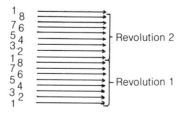

Fig. 10.1 Relationship of feeder to the course in circular machines.

Fig. 10.2 Alternating course variation on single system flat machines.

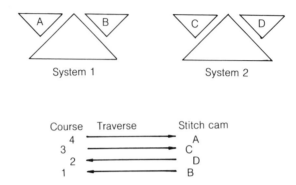

Fig. 10.3 Double system V-bed flat machines: (a) four cams producing courses; (b) course sequence.

due to course length variation, and measured for loop density. Weight per square metre would also be taken, to alert Quality Control to possible aberrations.

With circular machines the relationship of a particular feeder to the course it produces in the fabric is simple and consecutive (Fig. 10.1).

With flat machines the situation can be more complex, with knitting taking place from left to right and then right to left. A different set of cams on the machine produce the knitting left to right, than produce it right to left. On simple machines with one cambox/one yarn knitting the alternation is odd, even, odd, even etc. (Fig. 10.2), and a course length variation is expected to alternate.

On more complex knitting machines with two or more knitting systems traversing, the situation is more complex. On a two system V-bed flat machine there are four different groups of cams producing knitted courses A, B, C, D (Fig. 10.3). If the cam carriage is moving from right to left, the two trailing systems B, D are knitting, with B knitting the first course followed by D. When the carriage is moving from left to right A and C are knitting, with C knitting before A. In the fabric, the course sequence will be as shown in Fig. 10.3.

Recognition of this is essential when setting up a machine or locating a faulty source of course length distortion.

Weight per unit area and cover factor

Weight per unit area of fabric is an important property that is again related to a host of other properties. The 'weight' is determined by two factors that interact: the loop size and the yarn size. The effect of the loop size is simple to express: if the size of the yarn remains constant, then increase of loop size produces a decrease of weight per unit area. The effect is an inverse ratio.

Example

Let K = 20

$$S = \frac{K}{\ell^2}$$

(1) For a loop length of 0.4 cm:

$$S = \frac{20}{0.4^2} = 125 \text{ loops/cm}^2.$$

Length of yarn in 1 cm^2 of fabric = 125 × 0.4
= 50 cm

(2) For a loop length of 0.8 cm:

$$S = \frac{20}{0.8^2}$$
$$= 31.25 \text{ loops/cm}^2$$

Length of yarn in 1 cm^2 of fabric = 31.25 × 0.8
= 25 cm

So double the loop size means half the weight per square unit.

Usually in knitted fabrics, for fabrics of a similar construction, as loop length increases so the size of yarn increases. Yarn sizes are themselves expressed not in terms of diameter but in weight per unit length. This itself is an expression of volume. The relationship of a volume of a cylinder to its diameter can be reduced to that of the area of its cross section:

$$\text{area} = \pi\left(\frac{d}{2}\right)^2 \text{ or d is proportional to } \sqrt{\text{area}}$$

In a knitted fabric, to maintain cover, as the length of loop doubles so the diameter of the thread must double. Cover is a simple ratio of the area of a knitted fabric covered by yarn to the area covered by the gaps in between loops. It can be demonstrated that for a given knitted structure, if the cover ratio is maintained through a range of fabrics with different loop lengths, then those fabrics are related in characteristics of tightness/looseness and other physical properties.

This concept of cover leads to the property of 'normality' of a knitted fabric. A 'normal' fabric is one that is neither too tight and stodgy nor too loose and floppy. Lay observers given a range of fabrics of differing loop size and yarn size make surprisingly similar judgements on what 'normality' is in a knitted fabric intended for normal apparel.

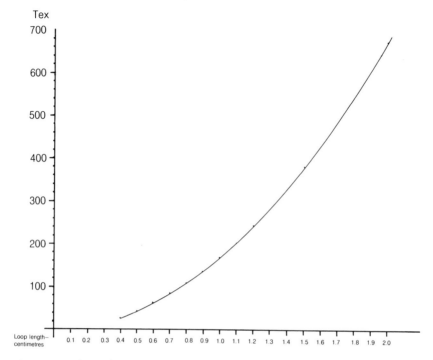

Fig. 10.4 Plain fabric: plot of yarn count in tex against loop length; $cf = \dfrac{\sqrt{tex}}{\ell} = 13$.

There is a simple formula that can be used to express 'cover factor' or tightness factor, taking into account and abbreviating diameter of yarn, length of loop and loop density.

$$\text{Cover factor (cf)} = \frac{\sqrt{\text{count in tex}}}{\ell} \qquad\qquad 2.$$

For a particular value of cover factor we can obtain a range of fabrics having similar normality relationships. It is possible to plot graphs for such relationships (Fig. 10.4) and for weight per square metre (Fig. 10.5).

The calculation for weight/m² involves combining the equation for loop density and the equation for cover factor:

Weight in gm of $1\,m^2$ of fabric

$$= \frac{\text{loops/cm}^2 \times \cancel{100}\,\text{cm} \times \cancel{100}\,\text{cm} \times \text{loop length}}{\cancel{100}\,\text{cm}} \times \frac{\text{tex}}{\cancel{1000}}$$

$$= \frac{\text{loops/cm}^2 \times \ell \times \text{tex}}{10}$$

As loops per $cm^2 = \dfrac{K}{\ell^2}$

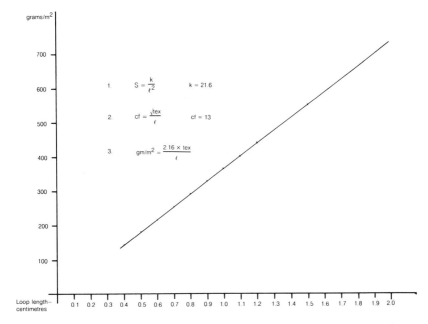

grams/m²

1. $S = \dfrac{k}{\ell^2}$ $k = 21.6$

2. $cf = \dfrac{\sqrt{tex}}{\ell}$ $cf = 13$

3. $gm/m^2 = \dfrac{2.16 \times tex}{\ell}$

Loop length–centimetres

Fig. 10.5 Plain fabric: weight/square metre against loop length.

$$\frac{K \times tex}{\ell \times 10} = \text{weight in gm of } 1\,m^2 \text{ of fabric} \qquad\qquad 3.$$

As $tex = (cf \times \ell)^2$

$$\frac{K \times (cf \times \ell)^2}{\ell \times 10} = \text{weight in gm of } 1\,m^2 \text{ of fabric} \qquad\qquad 4.$$

For the graph of weight per square metre against loop length, the values of 21.6 for K, and 13 for cf have been chosen.

The graph of the relationship between loop length and weight per square metre for a given construction while maintaining a cover factor, is a straight line, i.e. double the loop length, double the diameter of the yarn, double the weight/m². Specifications for knitted fabric usually include quantities for loop density, width of fabric and weight per m², and increasingly for loop length.

It has already been suggested in Chapter 4, when discussing cotton fabrics, that it is often difficult to measure dimensions and quantities because of the extensible nature of the material and the possibility that it is under stress at the time of measurement.

Measurements of fabric taken from a roll or lapped pile must always be considered to apply to the state that the fabric is in at the time of measurement. Unfortunately knitted fabric may change dimensions with time, handling and with subsequent wet treatments including steaming, and such changes can occur after the garment has been produced and sold to the public.

The concept of the relaxed state for knitted fabrics is well recognized and documented. Quality Control must ensure that before knitted garments are cut, the fabric is in a relaxed or near relaxed condition, i.e. that there will be little shrinkage of the fabric/garment when it is in the consumer's possession. Relaxation tests can be carried out on fabric as a routine procedure, or as spot checks on suspect deliveries. There are British Standard procedures for relaxation testing (BS 1955:1981(86) and BS 4736:1985), and some of the large retail/wholesale purchasers have established tests of their own. Most test procedures involve agitation in aqueous solution followed by measurement under water, and/or spinning and tumble drying. They attempt to reproduce the conditions under which the garment will be laundered during usage.

Cotton

The hydrophylic (water absorbing) fibres pose the greatest problems in fabric shrinkage or deformation, cotton being the major culprit in that it is readily distorted during knitting and wet processing. Cotton has little elastic recovery and so deformations remain until wetting and agitation swell and relax the fibres.

Wool

Wool is less of a problem, having good elastic properties. Very little wool fabric is now processed via the fully cut route, most being used in fully fashioned and stitch-shaped cut garments. Almost all wool knitted for apparel is shrink-resist finished, either in the yarn state or in the garment form.

Shrink resist treatment removes the potential for wool and other animal hairs to felt. Felting is induced by water and agitation, and is the result of the surface scales of the fibres acting as ratchets in irrecoverably consolidating the fabric. Such felting is used creatively in wool knitted garments to produce compact lofty fabrics in lambswool shetland styles. Shrink-resist finishing processes take place in this case after felting (milling). The process attacks the scales on the surface of the wool fabrics, damaging them sufficiently to prevent felting.

Steaming of knitted garment blanks or garments on an open steam bed releases the majority of stress in wool fabrics. Quality control is concentrated more on the efficacy of the shrink-resist processing. Testing is carried out to reproduce washing situations likely to be used by the consumer.

Acrylic fibres

Knitted fabrics made from acrylic fibres present few problems in dimensional stability; indeed this is considered one of their major assets. Acrylic piece goods are wet finished, but as they are hydrophobic (low

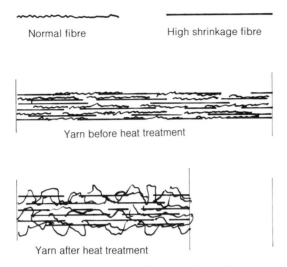

Fig. 10.6   Production of high bulk acrylic yarn.

water absorbing) fibres this has little or no effect on the dimensional
properties of the fabric; any distortions are induced mechanically or by
heat.

Mechanical distortion is possible on circular knitted fabric made from
acrylic fibres, although the final process in finishing is usually setting,
steaming or stentering, which either eliminate or stabilize such
distortions. The problem of quality control mostly centres on the degree
of distortion that has been induced and its regularity throughout the
fabric. Such distortion can involve uneven wale distribution across the
fabric, fabric skews of various types, and uneven course distribution
along the length of the fabric. The distortions produced during a heat
setting treatment are irrevocable and can make the fabric quite unusable
in cut garments. To test for purely mechanical distortions a short period
in a warm tumble-dryer will release most strains.

High bulk acrylic

Acrylic fibre is, in its high-bulk form, often used in knitted garments and
poses quality problems that are quite specific.

Acrylic fibre can be produced with a shrinkage potential, i.e. when such
fibres are exposed to heat they shrink in length by between 20% and
50%. Spinners can purchase a range of fibres with specific shrinkage
potential. Before spinning, normal no-shrink fibres are mixed with pro-
portions of high-shrink fibres. The yarn is spun on the worsted process
and then subjected to heat which makes the high shrinkage fibres decrease
in length, forming a core for the yarn and throwing the normal fibres up
to the surface of the yarn. This makes it very bulky and shrinks it by up
to 30% in length (Fig. 10.6).

The stage at which this can be carried out varies from continuous treatment immediately after spinning, through steam treatment in hank form to post knitting treatment in garment form.

Two quality problems arise from these processes:

(1) the processing has been uneven and results in barriness in various forms in the fabric or garment;
(2) the process has been inadequate or incomplete, resulting in shrinkage potential when the garment is exposed to subsequent heat treatment.

I have singled out the above three fibres in particular because they encapsulate the dimensional problems that knitted fabrics pose to the garment maker. There can also be quality problems with textured polyamide in swimwear and elastomerics in leisurewear, but essentially they are similar to those discussed.

Knitted faults

Knitted fabric has characteristic faults that occur as a result of the construction of the fabric. They can be categorized into horizontal and vertical components. One type of horizontal fault has already been outlined: that due to different course lengths being incorporated into the fabric.

Most other faults that result in horizontal barring are connected in some respect to the yarn used. These include:

- uneven counts between yarns;
- uneven counts within yarns;
- different dyeing shades between yarns;
- different dyeing within one yarn;
- different spinning/batch source of yarns;
- different bulking/heat treatment given to synthetic man-made yarns.

There are others specific to certain yarn and fibre types, but all these faults characterize themselves as bars across the fabric, of density, colour or lustre, and must be detected in the fabric before incorporation into the garment.

Vertical faults usually result from the knitting process but can occur with finishing. A common vertical fault is a needle line. At its most benign a faulty needle may produce a wale slightly larger or smaller, or distorted loops. Such lines may or may not result in the rejection of the fibre or garment, but they nevertheless produce an obvious lowering of its 'quality'.

Really faulty needles result in vertical lines of occasional or frequent tuck stitches, or occasional or frequent cut stitches where the yarn actually parts, with consequential holes. Tucking and cutting can sometimes occur at random, or through the whole piece, rendering it virtually useless.

In piece goods fabric produced on circular machines it is sometimes possible to split the fabric down a single bad wale line before finishing. Other solutions involve the messy business of removing damaged garment portions from the cut lay and re-cutting.

Such faults in garment blanks or fully fashioned panels render them unusable. In these industries it is much more likely that the knitter in control of the machines would notice them very early, and so prevent much wastage.

Stains

The knitting industry, unlike the weaving industry, uses oil to lubricate machinery in the immediate vicinity of where the fabric is being produced, i.e. on the needles themselves. Such oil mixed with atmospheric dust and metallic powder (swarf) can, in certain circumstances, cause stains on the fabric or garment being knitted. Two procedures are used to minimise this:

(1) control of the oil itself, by applying it in minimum quantities and delivering it continuously, so that it is present in the fabric but does not show up in any build up of soiled material that would result from spasmodic application;
(2) using oils that are readily mixed with water, so called scourable or clean oils.

The majority of knitted piece goods are wet-finished before cutting and there is little likelihood that oil staining will remain in finished fabric. On stitch-shaped garments it can present major problems if tight control is not exercised in the knitting room. As these garments are not generally wet finished, stains are usually dealt with during examination by solvent based spotting guns. The problem is negligible in the fully fashioned industry where oil is not used on the needles and where wet finishing is usual.

Stains due to oiling on knitted fabrics show as dirty areas, or horizontal marking associated with a particular course or group of courses, or vertical lines following one or more wales and fading away with distance.

Other stain characteristics of knitted fabric occur when accumulated lint (fibre dust) falls into knitting zones and gets incorporated into the fabric. Some circular machines are equipped with vacuum or blower devices to clear the immediate vicinity of the knitting zones. Such devices are not usual on flat machines and good housekeeping during the knitting process is essential.

Cleaning down is particularly important where the knitting of light-coloured fabric and garments occurs after the knitting of darker coloured ones. Similar problems occur if coloured fabrics/garment pieces are knitted in the same location as white or pastel coloured ones.

Lint staining in knitted fabric occurs in several forms, sometimes as concentrated 'blobs' thickening the fabric locally, or as strong horizontal lines, often occurring when the machine has remained stationary for a time. It also occurs as random flecks of dirt on a light-coloured fabric, or light flecks on a dark fabric. Such flecks often consist of a solitary fibre.

Some faults in knitted fabric and garments are only detected when the garment is in use. One such fault, common to all textiles, is fading of colour. This is well documented elsewhere and will not be dealt with here. Another common knitting problem, that occurs infrequently in woven fabrics, is pilling.

Pilling

Pilling is the formation on the surface of knitted fabrics of small balls of abraded fibre. It is connected with several factors:

(1) the type and size of fibre or fibre mixture used in the component yarn;
(2) the construction of the yarn in terms of twist factor;
(3) the type and tightness of knitted construction;
(4) the nature of the surface against which the knitted fabric has abraded.

The nature of the pills themselves is very interesting; they vary in size, distribution and density. Some only occur on areas of a garment associated with a particular movement, such as on the sides of an upper garment where the arms rub, or sometimes only on the upper chest and upper back where the garment is abraded by an outer garment.

Some pills consist only of fibres from the fabric on which they occur, others are 'robbed' from other garments. Such robbery is associated with fabrics knitted from textured polyester yarns, the abraded surface of which contains very strong fibres capable of entanglement.

This also highlights the fact that some pills are loosely attached and others strongly attached. Wool pills are considered weak and indeed sometimes drop off spontaneously. Pills produced in fabric containing polyamide or polyester fibres are considered strong and persist, making garments on which they occur unsightly and unwearable, even though not worn out.

Testing procedures involve tumbling samples in pill drums or pill boxes where they are abraded against both standard surfaces and against selected fabrics.

Summary

Fabric or garment portions at the start of the garment making process may exhibit the following undesirable, observable qualities:

(1)   the wrong construction, with loop length, width and weight per square metre variations from the specification;
(2)   variable loop length/course construction, showing horizontal barring;
(3)   horizontal barring from a number of yarn characteristics;
(4)   vertical faults that are machine determined;
(5)   stains due to oiling or lint contaminating the fabric.

All these observable faults are the subject of inspection procedures at the start of the garment making process. Some faults are not necessarily observable and have been discussed in relation to three of the common fibres used in knitting. Such faults relate to fabric stability and shrinkage or consolidation after being made into garments. The potential for shrinkage is sometimes indicated by abnormal measurements of loop density, but often can only be detected by testing.

Pilling, which is a particularly deleterious phenomenon in knitted garments, has also been discussed, with indications of the factors involved in its formation but no 'magic', one-off solution.

Garment quality

The quality of a knitted garment reflects all the processes through which the various components have passed during its manufacture.

Knitted fabric has already been discussed and the problems of quality outlined. Faults incurred during the knitting and fabric finishing processes pass on into the knitted garment itself unless detected and diverted. During the progress of the fabric or knitted pieces through the production system additional faults can be accumulated. The number of possible faults increases with the number of processes that a garment passes through. It follows, therefore, that fully cut garments have the greatest fault potential and some integral garments the least, with stitch-shaped cut and fully fashioned falling in between.

A man's sock cannot contain dimensional faults arising from cutting, nor multiple seaming problems. All the faults in a sock can be classified as knitting/yarn or dyeing/finishing. In contrast, on a fully cut garment, a dimensional aberration could be due to the knitted fabric, or the spreading/cutting, or the seaming, or the pressing. It follows that the quality control procedures of the production of fully cut garments need to be comprehensive and at all stages, to avoid cumulative faults.

A brief look at the stages that fully cut garments pass through, with observations on quality control procedures, will uncover most of the peculiarities of knitted garments.

Yarn assessment

Fabric for fully cut garments is mostly produced within the company itself and therefore the raw material itself is yarn. Where long term relationships have been established between the spinner and the garment manu-facturer, quality assurance is usually accepted as part of the relationship and testing of a delivered quality can be at a minimum. It would, however, be wrong to accept unquestioningly all deliveries, and periodic checks of quality are essential. Where deliveries of yarn are from various spinners, more intensive sampling and testing is required.

Testing implies that specifications have been established against which to test. Specification of incoming raw materials is one of the most neglected areas of knitting. Important factors to specify in knitting yarns are:

- count;
- count variability;
- evenness;
- singles and doubling twist;
- yarn strength;
- friction.

In some yarns characteristics associated with the particular fibres are important, such as fibre diameter (wool quality) in wool, the presence of trash and seed contamination in cotton, residual bulking in acrylic yarn, and crimp rigidity in textured polyester and polyamide yarns.

Some or all of the tests may be carried out routinely, while others may be only performed on suspect lots. The objective of maintaining yarn standards is to produce fabric that meets the specification laid down. All aberrations from yarn specifications produce measurable or visible faults within the fabric. Most of the testing procedures are outlined in BS Methods of Tests for Textiles.

Fabric assessment

Knitted fabric is usually examined at two stages: after knitting and after finishing. Quality control procedures are also carried out before and during knitting; before, to set the knitting machine to produce a par-ticular quality, and during to check that the quality is being maintained.

It is arguable that the 'knitter's' main function is quality control, to prevent the knitting machine producing faulty fabric. The rough exam-ination after knitting is to ensure that the fabric is not being produced with visible faults that by feedback can be rectified on a particular knitting machine. Some rough mending may be carried out to prepare the fabric for the dyeing and finishing process.

After finishing, the fabric is examined over an examination table, faults are identified and their location marked so that they can be dealt with during spreading or after cutting. Some firms mark only at the selvedge with a coloured tag, others locate the actual fault with a sticker as well.

Fault counts can be maintained to assess improving or deteriorating standards. Visual fault location cannot be 100%, neither can an operative act other than subjectively, and checks on the examiners also need to be carried out.

Spreading

The operatives who build up the fabric lay are also responsible for the quality control of the operation, whether they are spreading by hand or machine. For knitted fabrics in particular, general and localized stretching or distortion of the fabric must be avoided. Faults must be located and decisions made about them as regards eliminating them from the lay.

Alignment of features and patterns must be maintained where necessary and end wastage must be avoided. Also of great importance is ensuring that the number of layers in the entire lay, and the sub-numbers of particular colours or patterns, are correct. Again, procedures must be established to check that this is happening.

The accuracy of the marker and its positioning on the lay, or the marking of the pattern pieces on the top layer, must be the subject of close quality control. Dimensional problems can be induced at this stage, as can misalignments of garment portions or misalignments of patterns within or on the fabric. Another common mistake at this stage is to leave out one or more pieces of the garments.

It is also important to identify and label on the marker the relevant sizes of the garment portions, so that after cutting they are assembled in the correct bundles.

Cutting

When cutting by hand with straight knives it is very easy to deform knitted fabric, particularly within the depths of the lay. While the cutter is apparently following the surface marker, the lower layers are not necessarily being cut accurately.

Some fabrics are particularly difficult to cut, e.g. 1 × 1 rib, and the problem increases with depth of lay. There is also a strong element of cutter skill. Other faults of bad cutting are the failure to accurately follow lines of the marker, and the cutting off of corners.

Auto cutting and die cutting pose less of a problem but it must not be assumed that they are infallible. Constant checking by sampling must be carried out to ensure good standards.

Measures must be taken to ensure that the bundles assembled after cutting contain the correct number of pieces and that faulty pieces have been identified and compensated for. All the pieces must be for the same size garment.

Sewing

In Chapter 9 handling methods were discussed and it was suggested that the manner in which the sewing operation is organized has a direct bearing on quality problems. There is little doubt that division of labour accompanied by piece-rate work produces quality control headaches of a high order. In particular, knitted garments that are put together by overlocking pose problems.

The overlocking machinery actually cuts off the edge of the fabric to ensure a fixed dimension of bight. What is not fixed is the amount cut off. Patterns for knitted garments often contain an allowance for cutting by the overlock knives, which varies from 3 mm to 6 mm. A sloppy overlocker can readily cut 20 mm off a particular edge, altering the dimensions of the garment considerably.

Other problems arise from the difficulties of controlling alignment of two components during overlocking. Because knitted fabrics stretch it is easy for one of the components to stretch during seaming. Subsequent attempts at correction within the length of the seam make matters worse and the garment shows obvious distortions. Even slight misalignments at cuff and waistband ribs can be visually unacceptable.

The most difficult task for overlockers, cup seamers and flat seamers alike, is maintaining alignment of stripes or patterns on side seams. It is usual to select the most skilled operatives and to pay premium rates. Stripes and patterns are more usual on cut stitch shaped knitwear and overlockers in this industry gain the skills necessary to deal with them.

The other common problem with overlock seams in particular is distortion by general stretching during seaming. This shows as bowing or seam rippling. Some or all of this may be recoverable during finished steaming.

The above factors that affect quality, and need to be subject to control, relate to the operative and his/her skills of assembly. Such factors are best dealt with through training, environmental and management action rather than through checking, measurement and punitive action. The best quality control processes are built into the production system. 'Make well and there is little need to check'.

Other seaming factors relate to machine settings. Some customers specify stitches per centimetre or inch and this must be measured. The machine builder's graded marks are only approximations, not finite quantities. Where customers do not set the standard the manufacturer must set standards appropriate to his particular quality perception.

Seam balance is important in seams using more than one thread. For knitted garment seams this in particular means overlock seams and multithread chain stitches. It is strongly advocated that thread run in is used as an assessment of balance, rather than mere visual appearance. Run-in has already been discussed in Chapter 7 and its role in deciding the properties of a particular seam cannot be overstressed. The single and double chain stitch seams in particular, incorporated into collar seams, bear the load when the seam is stretched. Optimum values for thread run-in must be established and maintained to avoid customer complaints of seam failure.

Final inspection

All knitted garment manufacturers operate final inspection procedures to ensure that the quality they promise to customers is maintained. Analysis of the records of final inspections should also provide suggestions for action to improve quality. Examination results in garments being categorized into firsts, seconds and rejects.

Firsts pass through to packing. Seconds may be mended or the fault repaired in some other way, such as stain removal, loose thread tidying, debris removal etc. They move after another examination into first category. Likewise a major rejection fault may be overcome to move the garment into seconds category.

Very few companies allow absolute rejects to occur in their production process, and such events are usually associated with an unrecognized problem with the raw material, such as excessive pilling, dye fading, dye bleeding etc. Some faults, although measurable, are actually assessed visually. Examples include colour matching, colour variation between components, dimensional distortions and misalignments.

Other faults more obviously fall into the subjective category and pose difficulties in definition of their severity. Holes of all sizes usually result in rejection and may be subjected to mending that brings them into a seconds category. More difficult to categorize are flaws due to thick and thin localized irregularities in yarn that may occur in an inobvious place in the garment. Tidiness of make up is also judged at this stage, with loose sewing threads, debris and trailing overlock chains all tending to lower the perceived quality of the garment.

Such subjective judgements are not normally written into a garment specification but are covered by the premise that 'if the garment was passed and sold the customer would return it'. This leads to another concept – of different qualities for different customers. Manufacturers of knitted garments gain a feel for what a particular customer/market will tolerate, and adjust accordingly.

It is possible to overexamine, i.e. to reject too many garments. This can be as financially ruinous as allowing too many garments through that are sub-standard. Over examination results in garments, with which the layman can find no fault, being judged unacceptable and relegated to a seconds category.

Efficiency of examination

No examination process can be considered 100% effective, and observable or measurable faults creep through. Below 80% the examination process could be regarded as inefficient. There is a time factor involved, in that efficiencies rise with time spent on examination. Indeed efficiency can be estimated by withdrawing samples of garments examined and subjecting them to a much more thorough examination, i.e. spending more time on the job.

The other factor involved with efficiency is the simple and obvious premise that 'the bigger and more obvious the particular fault, the less likely it is to escape examination'. Examiners are assessed and trained on collections of garments with particular faults. It is also wise to have group discussions with examiners when changes of style, production process, raw materials and customer specification takes place, to establish peculiarities in the standards asked for.

Dimensional considerations

Measuring the dimensions of knitted garments poses particular problems. These have already been aired earlier in this chapter. The act of measuring itself is difficult. Handling and placing a knitted garment on a flat surface can induce stretch of up to 5%.

The edges of knitted garments can be indeterminate and of a rounded fold rather than a precise, crisp edge. Tolerances of width measurement need to be generous and related to more absolute quantities such as a total number of wales.

Widths of the waistbands, cuffs, collars and facings of knitwear are commonly expressed in terms of the number of ribs, but only on the coarsest gauges can the ribs be counted economically during production.

It is usual on upper body garments to measure routinely at examination the body width at under arm, total length, length of each sleeve underarm and width of each shoulder. Again the skill of the examiner in placing the garment on the table and in using the rule is vital. Examiners can be said to sense rather than measure a garment that is out of specification.

Weight

Weight of a garment can be used as a quality control measure to assess overall variability. It is particularly useful in the fully fashioned industry and in quality control of integral garments such as $\frac{1}{2}$ hose. Used in conjunction with control charts it enables a selection to be made of garments that fall outside control limits, for further examination.

Weight control charts also highlight dangerous trends towards higher or lower limits that occur in production processes.

Weight is also useful during production to assess the variability of the cutting process and of garment length or piece knitting. In such usage the two interacting factors of yarn size and loop length are being assessed as well as the state of relaxation.

Quality assurance

A chapter on quality control cannot be complete without mentioning the major influence that the British Standards Institute have had in establishing standards and test procedures, not only for British industry but in its contribution to the International Standard Organisation.

Of particular importance is the British Standard in Quality Assurance itself. BS 5750 is part of a wide range of quality standards that are assembled in BS Handbook 22, first published in 1981: 'This International Standard specifies quality system requirements for use where a contract between two parties requires the demonstration of a supplier's capability to design and supply product. The requirements specified in this International Standard are aimed primarily at preventing non-conformity at all stages from design through to servicing'.

Firms can in fact be registered as conforming to BS 5750 by complying with all the requirements and submitting to a 'quality audit' by one of the consultant companies authorised by the BSI. Registration brings rewards in the UK of being a recognised supplier to Governmental buying organisations, as well as bringing assurance to customers of the firm of the ability to supply 'quality'.

The international element is covered by BS 5750 parts 1, 2 and 3 being identical to ISO 9000, 9001, 9002, 9003, 9004 (1987). The contents of BS 5750 are a guide to good practice from the design stage and specification through to final inspection, with advice on inspection, supplying, keeping records, training, internal auditing, quality procedures and good practice in drawing up contracts and dealing with customers' requirements.

Good quality control practices reap rewards in terms of greater market demand for goods, less wastage due to rejection and down grading during production, fewer returns by ultimate customers and less loss of confidence by those who do not return goods but are nevertheless dissatisfied.

Design factors

In any market dealing with clothing, visual design itself is considered a quality. It must be recognized that hitting the right design for the market often overrides considerations by the ultimate customer of such factors as durability, fitness for purpose, neatness of make up and other utilitarian factors.

Good design must be considered a very important tool in the armoury of quality assurance.

Glossary

Barriness: visual banding on weft knitted fabrics caused by a number of different factors. Usually such bars are horizontally disposed, i.e. the course direction.

Bartack: an intensely concentrated zig-zag stitch forming a band 2–4 mm wide by 1–2 cm long, used to strengthen pocket edges, placket edges, waistband seams and cuff seams.

Bearded needle (Fig G1): a needle formed of one piece of spring steel needing the assistance of sinkers and pressers to form loops.

Bight, bite: the distance from the edge of a fabric or fabrics that the needle thread penetrates in an overedge seam construction.

Bobbin: a small flanged cylinder around which the bobbin thread is wound. Such bobbins are a basic element in lockstitch machines and are caused to pass through a loop formed by the needle thread, thus twisting the two threads together at each stitch.

Bundle: a collection of sufficient pieces of cut fabric to make up several garments. The size of the bundle is limited by weight and the number of pieces required for each garment.

CAD: acronym for computer-aided design. Used to describe the stages whereby a computer is used to assist in the designing of a product.

CAM: short for computer-aided manufacture. Used to describe processes of making a product where the production machine is controlled by a computer.

Casting off: a sealed edge to the last course of a piece of knitting, created by chaining a separate thread through each of the loops of the last course. This is normally regarded as a hand technique but recently automatic casting off has been achieved on models of Shima Seiki flat knitting machines.

Circular knitting machine: a machine in which the needle bed is either cylindrical or a circular disc. In the first the needles are situated

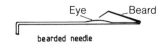

Fig. G1   (above) Bearded needle.

Fig. G2   (right) Closed loop.

vertically in grooves formed in the outer surface of the cylinder. In the second the needles are situated horizontally in grooves radially cut in the upper surface of the disc. Circular rib machines have both cylinder and dial. Plain machines have cylinder only.

Chain stitch: stitches formed by interlooping one or more threads.

Closed loop (Fig G2): a term used in both weft and warp knitting to describe a loop closed at the base, i.e. the component thread crosses over itself in the construction of the loop.

Consecutive knitting: a term used to describe the act of loop formation along a row, one loop at a time. This is a characteristic of most weft knitting machines using the latch needle, and also describes hand knitting. In contrast, flat bearded needle machines incorporate loops into the fabric collectively.

Course: a row of loops essentially formed from one or very few threads running from side to side of a weft knitted fabric. In machine knitting it is the product of one knitting cycle.

Course length: the length of yarn in one whole course of a fabric with selvedges, or one whole circumference of a circular fabric. It may be expressed as the length of yarn in a given number of loops, usually 100, or multiples or factors of 100.

Cover (seams): the extent to which an overedge seam covers up the raw cut edge of a fabric or fabrics.

Cover factor, tightness factor: a measure of the relationship between the loop length of a knitted fabric and the size/count of the yarn employed to construct it. A range of fabrics of differing loop size are considered to have related properties if the yarn size increases to maintain the same cover factor.

The usual formula is:

$$\text{cover factor} = \frac{\sqrt{\text{count in tex}}}{\text{loop length}}$$

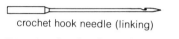
crochet hook needle (linking)

Fig. G3 Crochet hook needle (linking).

Crimp tester: a device consisting of two clamps that can trap each end of a 'crimped' piece of thread. The clamps are slid apart until a certain loading is achieved, and the length of the thread is then ascertained. The crimp tester is used in the analysis of knitted fabrics, to measure course length and loop length.

Crochet hook needle (linking) (Fig. G3): a type of needle in the form of a crochet hook used on linking machinery to drag loops of thread through the work.

Cuttled *see* **Flopped**

De-skilled linking machine: a certain type of machine with a point dial on to which work is randomly run. The machine produces a single or double chain stitch in a similar manner to a normal conventional needle linking machine. Sometimes such machines produce twin single chain stitch, and they may have an edge cutter. The de-skilling reflects the fact that the operative is not required to run each loop of the work on to a point of the dial.

De-skilled overlocker: a machine having a point dial on to which the work is precisely run on. As the dial revolves the fabric is joined first by a single chain stitch, followed by cutting the fabric edge at a pre-determined bight, followed by seaming with a three thread overlock stitch. The machine both de-skills the overlocking task and enables difficult patterned fabrics to be joined with precision.

Dial (linking): A circular metal plate with grooved points round the edge facing radially outwards at a pre-determined frequency (gauge), related to the loop density of the work to be seamed.

Differential feed (sewing): a work advancing mechanism where the dogs are divided into two groups, one before the needle(s) and one after. The two groups are capable of advancing the work at different rates. If the front group advances the work faster than the rear, a condition of compression or overfeed will occur. If the front group advances the work at a slower rate than the rear, a condition of stretching or underfeed will occur. In knitted garment production differential feed is used to lessen stretching of the fabric during seaming.

Digital socks: knitted foot coverings in which a single tube covering the ankle and instep of the foot splits into more than one tube at the toes. The tubes fit over one or more toes.

Dogs, feed-dogs: toothed metal devices positioned under or over the work that advance the fabric components during stitching. Under work they form an oval movement, at the top of which they protrude through the throat plate and move forward, advancing the fabric one stitch; then they sink below the throat plate and return to their original location.

Domestic knitting machine: a knitting machine designed to be used in the home. In spite of this the machines can be very complex and versatile. Most types feature some form of needle selection and some types have computer controls. These machines have been widely used industrially, particularly by designer-led high fashion firms.

Double jersey (rib) knitting machine: a machine, usually circular, having two sets of needles disposed at 90° to one another, and used for the production of piece goods in rib fabric.

Drop shoulder: the shape of the junction between the sleeve and the body of a garment, where the junction runs between the underarm point and a position below the extreme end of the shoulder, i.e. on the upper arm itself.

Facing: an additional piece of fabric attached to the upper surface of a garment. Usually used in knitted garments at the front joining edges of cardigans and jackets, but also used to describe the button-stands of neck openings of shirt style garments.

Fashioning angle: the angle formed at the edge of a piece of fashioned fabric, measured between course alignment and the line of the fashioned selvedge.

Fashioning frequency: the number of courses between two succeeding fashionings within a series.

Feed-dogs *see* **Dogs**

Feeder: the collective mechanisms on a knitting machine that produce a course of loops. Confusingly the term is also used to describe the metal plate with a hole or holes, that guides the yarn into the hooks of latch needles during loop formation. Both terms are commonly used in relation to circular machines, which are classified according to the number of feeders they possess. This defines the maximum number of courses they can knit in one revolution of the machine.

Flèchage (course shaping): a term increasingly used to define two and three dimensional shaping of knitted fabric by increasing and/or decreasing the length of succeeding knitted courses to a pre-planned series. Beret knitting is also a term used to describe this process. The term is derived from the French for wedge.

Flopped: a form of packaging of a long length of fabric. The fabric is folded backwards and forwards on itself over a dimension between 0.6 m and 1 m. The finished form is like a rectangular box. Flopped fabric is considered to be in a more relaxed state than rolled fabric and is therefore the desirable packaging form for knitted fabric even though it presents transportation difficulties unless wrapped.

Fully-cut: a class of knitted garment derived from piece goods. All the edges of the pieces of the garment are cut.

Fully fashioned: garments constructed from pieces of weft knitted fabric with perfect selvedges. The shapes of the pieces are generated by movement of loops at the edges to diminish or enlarge the width of the fabric.

Garment blank *see* **Knitted blank**

Gauge: the linear spacing of needles in the bed or bar of a knitting machine. Expressed as needles per inch, needles per 1.5 in, or as a number of millimetres per 10 tricks (needle spaces). Imperial measure is commonly used world-wide.

'Griege' state: unfinished, natural fibre, yarn or fabric. Most commonly used in conjunction with cotton.

Grinning (seams): the gap when two components stitched together are pulled apart laterally. The gap will be larger when the stitch is slacker, i.e. the run-in ratio of the threads is larger.

Half-gauging: removing alternate needles from a knitting machine either physically or by selection, to coarsen the gauge or to enable certain loop manipulations to take place.

Half-hose: a leg covering ending at mid-calf.

Hand flat knitting machine: a V-bed, flat bed or single bed latch needle knitting machine designed to be powered by hand. Such machines are widely used industrially, where the product competes favourably with the power machine. Very quick response and very short production runs are possible.

Hand-frame: knitting machines constructed like the original invented by the Reverend William Lee in Calverton (1589), having horizontally mounted bearded needles and drop down sinkers. A characteristic of the hand frame is the heavy oak 'frame' that supports the working 'head'.

Hose: a total leg covering ending in a position above the knee.

Intarsia: a knitted fabric in which there are solid areas of colour patterning. The characteristic of such areas is that they consist only of the yarn forming them; no other coloured yarn passes either through them or behind them. Joins between the areas of colour are formed either by entwining the sinker loops of adjacent areas or by plating adjacent area loops.

Integral or integrally knitted garments: weft knitted garments constructed so that they require little or no cutting, and little or no seaming operations to finish them.

Jersey fabric: a loose term used to describe weft knitted piece goods. *Single jersey* – plain weft knitted fabric or modified plain weft knitted fabric, used as piece goods. *Double jersey* – rib weft knitted fabric or modified rib weft knitted fabric, used as piece goods.

Knitted blank or garment blank: a piece of fabric from which a garment portion or portions are cut, and whose width and length relates to that garment portion. It also incorporates shaping by changes of stitch size or type. Invariably the lowest edge, the bottom of the blank, is a welt.

Knitted fabric: a fabric constructed from intermeshed loops.

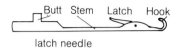

latch needle

Fig. G4 (above) Latch needle.

Knitted loop: a single unit of weft knitted fabric intermeshed above and below with different threads, and usually sharing the same thread with the loops on either side. *Face loop* – a simple open loop pulled through the loop below it towards the viewer. *Back loop* – a simple open loop passed through the loop below it away from the viewer.

Knitting: the action of forming fabrics by the intermeshing of loops.

Latch needle (Fig. G4): a needle formed of two parts, a butted hook and a swinging latch, capable of forming loops independent of other elements.

Lay: a build up of two or more layers of fabric so that they can be cut collectively into garment portions. The dimensions of the lay in respect of number of layers and length are pre-determined, as is the layout of the garment pieces on the upper surface of the lay.

Laying up or spreading: the act of building the lay from rolls or piles of fabric.

Lockstitch: stitches formed by the twisting of two or more threads together within the depth of a seam.

Loop density: the number of loops within an area of fabric expressed as loops per cm^2 or loops per in^2.

Looper: an element on chain stitch machines that is instrumental in forming loops but does not pass through the fabric being seamed. Loopers may themselves carry threads that form loop series or may simply aid the formation of needle loops.

Loop length: the length of yarn in one loop of a simple weft knitted fabric, usually expressed as an average of several or many measured loops.

Main shaft: most sewing machines are belt driven and the driver pulley is attached to a shaft in the machine. This is the main shaft and from its rotation all the movements of the mechanisms are derived.

Marker: a pre-determined cutting plan on paper or in a computer memory, that is placed on top of the lay to determine the location of pieces of garment and to guide the cutter.

Mock linking: a use of random linking where linking is normally used, such as collar attachment, the intention being to make the seam appear to have been linked while gaining a faster speed along with a certain amount of de-skilling.

Multi thread chain stitches (interlock stitches, covering stitches): a

Fig. G5 (right) Open loop.

versatile group of stitch types forming flat seams. Two to four needle thread chain stitching in a parallel formation is joined together on one side of the fabric by interlooping with a single thread. The other side of the stitching may also be joined by one or more threads known as covering threads. The classification of such seams is confused in that they fall into two groups within the BS/ISO system.

Narrowing: a movement of loops inwards at the selvedge of a piece of fabric. The result is a decrease in the number of loops in the succeeding course. The term is used to describe the action of carrying this out and the actual site of it.

Open loop (Fig. G5): in both weft and warp knitting a loop open at the base, i.e. the component thread does not cross over itself in the construction of the loop.

Overlock (overedge, overchain): stitches used to bind the edges of fabric to prevent them fraying. In knitted garments such stitches are also used to form seams between two or more fabrics. Invariably overlock describes the looped stitch construction formed from two or more threads, although overedge stitches can be achieved with a single chaining thread and with zig-zagged lockstitch.

Pattern cutter: a person who determines the shapes of the components of garments, to ensure that they fit together and, when assembled, reflect the intentions of the designer. They must also conform to the dimensions of the intended size.

Piece-rate: a method of payment of employees by pricing the task that they are required to do. The more tasks they complete within a certain time, the higher the reward.

Pilling: the formation of small nodules of compacted loose fibre (pills) on the surface of a fabric. Such pills result from abrasion of the fabric. Their severity is measured by density on the surface, but they may vary in relative strength of attachment, in size and in colour. In the latter, the pills may accumulate fibres from external sources.

Plain weft knitted fabric: the simplest construction of weft knitting in which the loops are all of one sort, open loops, and are all intermeshed in the same manner. (See diagrams Chapter 2).

Plated fabric: a knitted construction in which two yarns appear in every loop. They are arranged so that one appears only on the face of each loop and the other appears only on the back. Patterns may be achieved by reversing the front/back role of the yarn (reverse platings).

Plating: the action of producing plated fabric.

Point-lace: a knitted form of lace or open-work fabric made on a hand frame using loop transfer techniques. This fabric was one of the main products of the Nottingham trade in the 18th century, following the introduction of cotton yarns.

Polo collar: a variation of the round neck collar on a jumper, that extends well up the neck and is turned over or doubled on the outside.

Positive feed (knitting): a system often fitted to circular knitting machines to positively drive the yarn at a fixed rate relative to the surface speed of the needle cylinder. By this means uniform course lengths between feeders can be obtained, as well as constant course length throughout production.

Presser foot (knitting): a device for controlling loop formation that operates in the knitting zone of a rib or plain machine, and diminishes the need for take down weight on the fabric as it is formed. Plates and wires of various sorts are used for this purpose.

Presser foot (sewing): a device for holding the fabric components of a seam in place and against the advancing dogs during stitching.

Pressing off: the act of removing knitting from the needles of a knitting machine. This may be by design at the end of or progressively during a knitting cycle, or by accident when the yarn breaks during knitting.

Production line: a linear arrangement of sewing machines, each dedicated to a limited task within the production of a garment. The number of machines devoted to a particular task is related to the proportion of time that the task occupies in the total time required to produce the garment. The work usually passes from one operative to another in bundles.

Purl weft-knitted fabric: if a fabric contains both back and face loops in any one wale then it is a purl fabric.

Quick response: diminishing the time between ordering and delivery to the minimum.

Rack, racking: the movement of one knitting bed of a rib or purl knitting machine relative to the other, either to produce deflections within the fabric being knitted or to re-align the elements for a different structure to that previously being knitted.

Partial racking, i.e. less than one full needle space, may be required to facilitate loop transfer from one bed to the other on a rib machine.

Raglan sleeve: the shape of the junction between the sleeve and the body of a garment, in which the junction appears on both back and front of the garment as a straight line running between the underarm and a point on the neckline of the garment. The term is used in both woven and knitted garment construction.

Random linking: the joining of two pieces of fabric by a chain stitch, the stitch density of which exceeds the loop spacing density of the fabric being joined, the intention being that at least every loop across the fabric is penetrated by at least one loop.

Relaxed state (knitted fabric): the dimensional state of a fabric when the forces within the loop structure are in equilibrium and it is considered that the fabric can consolidate no more, without the application of force.

Rib weft-knitted fabric: a construction in which all the loops in any one wale are all the same, either back loops or face loops. However the loops are mixed back and face within the fabric (see diagrams in Chapter 2). The appearance of the fabric is reminiscent of animal ribs, hence the name.

Robotics: the complete replacement of human beings in a handling situation. The application of robotics to the making of garments proves very difficult because of the flexible nature of the materials.

Round neck collar: a collar on a jumper that encircles the lower part of the neck, without being either loose or tight.

Run-in: the length of thread absorbed into a known length or number of stitches in warp knitting, weft knitting and seaming.

Run-in ratio (seams): the ratio between a given length of seam and the length of one of the threads consumed in creating it. In a complex stitch involving several threads there will be several run-in ratios. The most useful ones involve the needle threads.

Running-on: the placing of previously knitted loops, or a selvedge, back on to the needles of a knitting machine for the addition of a further piece of knitting. The term is also used when an intermediate transfer bar is used to run on to, as in placing the waistband and cuff ribs on to a straight bar knitting machine when knitting fully fashioned garments.

Saddle shoulder: the shape of the junction between the sleeve and the body of a garment where the line starts at the underarm, progresses as

selvedge; weft knitting

Fig. G6   Selvedge, weft knitting.

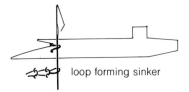

loop forming sinker

Fig. G7 Loop forming sinker.

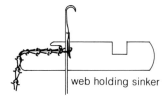

web holding sinker

Fig. G8 Web holding sinker.

a set-in or raglan to a point approximately two thirds up the armhole, then changes to a line parallel to the shoulder itself. The sleeve head has a tongue projection to achieve this.

Seams: the term used to describe the composite result of fabric being stitched. Taken into account are the relationship between the stitching and the edges of the fabric(s), the particular folding of the fabric, the entry location of the needle in stitching, and the positions of looper and seam covering threads. Seams are categorised by five figure numbers in the BS/ISO classification.

Selvedge (Fig. G6): the sealed edge of a piece of weft knitted fabric. The edge is formed when the thread forming a course turns back at the edge of the knitting and is used to create the succeeding course. The term is derived from weaving where the weft thread also turns back to form succeeding picks.

Set-in sleeve: the shape of the junction between the sleeve and the body of a garment, where the line runs from the underarm to the apparent top of the extreme end of the shoulder. The term is used in both woven and knitted garment construction.

Single jersey (plain web) knitting machines: a machine, usually circular, with a single set of needles, used for the production of piece goods on a plain fabric basis.

Sinkers: mechanisms that assist needles in forming loops, either by directly pushing a measured length of yarn around needles (loop forming sinkers, Fig. G7), or by supporting the already formed knitted fabric during loop formation and preventing the fabric rising as the needles rise during the knitting cycle (web holding sinkers, Fig. G8). All types consist of shaped thin metal plates situated between, and alternating with, needles.

Spirality: a distortion of a knitted fabric whereby the wales and courses align at an angle other than 90°. This condition is usually caused by residual torque in the component yarns.

Spreader: a device for manipulating fabric to form the layers of a lay. It may vary from primitive hand-moved types to sophisticated fully automatic machines.

Spreading *see* **Laying up**

Statement (fully fashioned knitting): a written programme describing the events required to knit a portion of a fully fashioned garment sequentially.

Stenter: a dry or steam heated oven of controlled temperature through which fabric is passed stretched between lines of pins. The object is to give the fabric particular dimensions of length and width, and to eliminate creasing. Thermoplastic fibre fabrics achieve a 'set'.

Stitch (sewing): the geometric configuration of threads used to produce a particular seam. Stitches may be used to join pieces of fabric or to produce a decorative effect. They are classified according to their geometric configuration and are placed into six categories within the BS/ISO system.

Stitch density: the number of repeats of the stitch per unit length of the seam, expressed as stitches per centimetre or stitches per inch.

Stitch-shaped cut: a class of knitted garment derived from knitted blanks. The dimensions of the blank are determined by the sizes of the garment portions to be cut from it.

Stolling: a knitted strip used as a facing, in which the wales run along the length.

Straight-bar knitting machine: a type of knitting machine equipped with vertically disposed bearded needles mounted in a bar. Loop formation is aided by loop forming sinkers, knock over bits and pressers. Machines are actually made with a number of 'heads', each head consisting of a needle bar with its attendant sinkers and capable of producing a single piece of garment. It is this machine that is used to produce the majority of fully fashioned garments, most of which are knitted in plain fabric.

Take down: a device on a knitting machine that ensures that fabric is removed from the knitting machine at a constant linear rate or at a constant tension.

Tex: a measurement of the size of a yarn, defined as the weight in grams of 1000 metres of the yarn. Tex is the internationally accepted sizing system.

Throat plate: the metal plate supporting the work in the stitching zone. Slots are cut in the plate through which the dogs protrude, holes are located for needle passage to the bobbin or loopers below the plate, and extensions of the plate are used for chaining fingers on the overlock and multithread chain stitch machines.

Tightness factor *see* **Cover factor**

Timing diagram: an analysis of the movements of the parts of a machine in time. In the examples used in this book the timing is in the form of one rotation of the main shaft, during which one stitch is formed.

Toile: a trial garment that tests the shape, dimensions and finishes of the design and enables alterations to be made at an early stage.

Turtle neck collar: a variation of the round neck collar that extends a moderate way up the neck and is not normally doubled over.

Unroving: the pulling out of a row of knitting or seam stitching by disconnecting the constituent loops in a chain reaction. All weft knitted constructions will unrove from the end last knitted and all chain stitch seams will unrove from the end last formed.

V-bed knitting machine: a flat knitting machine with two linear needle beds inclined, facing one another at an approximate angle of 90°.

V-neck collar: a collar on a jumper that dips at the front of the body into a V-shape. The length of the V below the neckline can vary considerably.

Wale: an intermeshed row of loops running from end to end of a weft knitted fabric. In machine knitting it is the product of one needle.

Wale shaping: two and three dimensional shaping of knitted fabric achieved by the movement of wales, which are both terminated and introduced to a pre-determined plan.

Waste factor: the amount of material left when garment portions are cut from piece goods, knitted blanks or shaped garment portions. The waste is expressed as a percentage of the weight of the original fabric.

Weft knitted fabric: fabric in which the constituent threads generally pass from side to side of the fabric, along the advancing line of construction. A course of such a fabric normally consists of one or very few threads.

Welt: a term employed to describe a stable knitted structure used at the extremities of a knitted article where the fabric is not incorporated into a seam. The function of the welt is to prevent the edge of the fabric from unroving, laddering and distorting after stretching. Welts particularly occur at hems, waistbands, cuffs, collars and facings.

Widening: a term used to describe the movement of loops outwards at the selvedge of a piece of fabric. The result of such movement is an increase in the number of loops in the succeeding course (usually by one loop), thus widening the fabric. The term is used both to describe the action itself and the site of it.

Work in progress: the amount of work within the production process. This is related to the production technique employed and to the efficiency with which it is managed. Work in progress is expected to rise in proportion to total output.

Yarn speed meter: an instrument for measuring the speed of yarn entering a circular knitting machine at a particular feeder. By combining this with a knowledge of the speed of the machine and the number of needles it contains, a mean loop size can be calculated.

Zig-zag stitch: stitches formed by alternating the location of penetration of the needle on either side of a lengthwise band of stitching. The stitch generally used is lockstitch.

Bibliography

Aldrich, W. (1992) *CAD in Clothing and Textiles*. Blackwell Scientific Publications, Oxford.

Aldrich, W. (1977) *Metric Pattern Cutting*. Unwin Hyman Ltd, London.

Blackner J. (1815, republished 1985) *The History of Nottingham*. The Amethyst Press, Otley, Yorkshire.

British Association of Clothing Machinery Manufacturers (1989) *The Cloth Cutting Machine – a History*. London.

British Standards Institution, Milton Keynes.
  BS 3870 Parts 1 & 2: 1982 Stitches and Seams.
  BS 6441: 1977 Methods of Tests for Knitted Fabrics.
  BS 1955: 1981(86) ⎱ Methods of Relaxation
  BS 4736: 1985 ⎰ of Knitted Fabrics.
  BS Handbook 22: Quality Assurance.

Carr H. & Latham B. (1988) *The Technology of Clothing Manufacture*. Blackwell Scientific Publications, Oxford.

Chapman S. (Ed) (1989) *Four Centuries of Machine Knitting*. Knitting International, Leicester.

Farrands C. and Totterdil P. (1990) *Markets, Production and Machinists in Nottinghamshire's Clothing and Knitwear Industries*. Nottinghamshire County Council, Nottingham.

Felkin W. (1967) *History of the Machine Wrought Hosiery and Lace Manufacturers*. David & Charles, Newton Abbot, Devon.

Fitton R.S. (1989) *'The Arkwrights', Spinners of Fortune*. Manchester University Press, Manchester.

Henson G. (1833, republished 1968) *The Civil, Political and Mechanical History of the Framework Knitting*. David & Charles, Newton Abbot, Devon.

Johnson-Hill B. (1978) *Fashion Your Future*. The Clothing Institute, London.

Knitting International. *Report from the Select Committee on Framework*

Knitters Petition. The House of Commons 1 April 1819. Reprinted by Knitting International, Leicester.

Mills R.W. (1965) *Fully Fashioned Garment Manufacture*. Cassell, London.

Modig N. (1988) *Hosiery Machines, Their Development, Technology and Practical Use*. Meisenback, Bamberg.

Palmer M. (1984) *Framework Knitting*. Shire Publications Ltd, Aylesbury, Buckinghamshire.

Pearson M. (1984) *Traditional Knitting*. Collins, London.

Spencer D. (1989) *Knitting Technology*. Pergamon Press, Oxford.

Taylor P. (1990) *Computers in the Fashion Industry*. Heinemann Professional Publishing, Oxford.

Textile Institute (1989) *Textile Terms and Definitions* 8th ed. The Textile Institute, Manchester.

Thomis M.I. (1969) *Politics and Society in Nottingham 1785–1835*. Basil Blackwell, Oxford.

Index

Also available from Blackwell Science Ltd

Metric Pattern Cutting
Third Edition
Winifred Aldrich
The number one, best-selling book on pattern
cutting for women's wear, including a new
section on computerised pattern cutting and
numerous blocks.
192 pages, illustrated hardback.
ISBN 0 632 03612 5

Metric Pattern Cutting for Menswear
Including Computer Aided Design
Third Edition
Winifred Aldrich
In the third edition of this standard work on the
subject, sizing charts have been updated and the
chapter devoted to computer-aided design has
been updated and extended. An extra section on
workwear has been added.
160 pages, illustrated hardback.
ISBN 0 632 04113 7

**Metric Pattern Cutting for Children's
Wear** From 2–14 years
Second Edition
Winifred Aldrich
Another bestseller by Winifred Aldrich,
providing a simple but comprehensive system of
pattern cutting for children's wear. Highly
illustrated with hundreds of stylish diagrams
and clear, concise instructions.
165 pages, illustrated hardback.
ISBN 0 632 03057 7

**Pattern Cutting for Lingerie,
Beachwear and Leisurewear**
Ann Haggar
Describes the whole process from planning to
finished pattern pieces. Includes examples,
working diagrams and drawings and patterns
for stretch fabrics.
250 pages, illustrated paperback.
ISBN 0 632 02033 4

Dress Pattern Designing The Basic
Principles of Cut and Fit
Fifth Edition
Natalie Bray
With Fashion Supplement by Ann Haggar
This classic book contains over 100 basic
diagrams and 40 plates, combined with clear,
detailed instructions.
192 pages, illustrated paperback.
ISBN 0 632 01881 X

More Dress Pattern Designing
Fourth Edition
Natalie Bray
With Fashion Supplement by Ann Haggar
Expands the basic course, applying the
principles and methods to more advanced styles
and specialist cutting techniques. Includes
lingerie, tailoring and children's patterns.
208 pages, illustrated paperback.
ISBN 0 632 01883 6

Dress Fitting
Second Edition
Natalie Bray
Discusses fitting problems including techniques
for better fit; problems of figure, posture and
pattern adjustment; identifying and dealing with
a defect.
120 pages, illustrated paperback.
ISBN 0 632 01879 8

Pattern Grading for Women's Clothes
The Technology of Sizing
Gerry Cooklin
Provides over 50 demonstrations of master and
basic garment grades, simple, clear instructions,
200 illustrations and 30 detailed charts of
international sizing systems.
400 pages, illustrated paperback.
ISBN 0 632 02295 7

**Pattern Grading for Children's
Clothes** The Technology of Sizing
Gerry Cooklin
Includes demonstration grades broken down
into illustrated stages with simple, clear
instructions, and children's size charts from
Europe and the USA.
320 pages, illustrated paperback.
ISBN 0 632 02612 X

Pattern Grading for Men's Clothes
Gerry Cooklin
A comprehensive manual of the practical
principles and applications of pattern grading
for the whole range of men's clothing, including
computerised grading, latest developments in
fully automatic grading and grades for linings,
fusibles and pockets.
304 pages, illustrated paperback.
ISBN 0 632 03305 3

Master Patterns and Grading for Women's Outsizes
Gerry Cooklin
Improved foundation garments and greater fashion awareness make it imperative for an entirely new approach to the construction and sizing of garment patterns for outsizes. This new textbook is a specialised and up-to-date treatment of the subject, and provides pattern cutters and graders with a wealth of practical information.
128 pages, illustrated paperback.
0 632 03915 9

Pattern Cutting for Women's Outerwear
Gerry Cooklin
Highly illustrated with clear stage-by-stage instructions, this innovative book emphasises the technological aspects of pattern development for women's mass-produced clothing. A simple, integrated system of drafting block patterns is described, followed by a wide-ranging toolbox of professional pattern cutting techniques with many examples of their applications. Patterns for linings and fusibles and computerised pattern design systems are also described.
192 pages, illustrated paperback.
0 632 03797 0

The Technology of Clothing Manufacture
Second Edition
Harold Carr & Barbara Latham
Includes cutting, sewing, alternative methods of joining materials and pressing; manual, mechanical and computer-controlled methods of production ; current applications of computerised techniques and robotics.
288 pages, illustrated paperback.
ISBN 0 632 03748 2

Understanding Fashion
Elizabeth Rouse
Highly illustrated, this book investigates the social and cultural significance of clothing and fashion, the influence that social changes have on styles of dress and on the development of the fashion industry and why and how fashion as we know it today has developed.
320 pages, illustrated paperback.
0 632 01891 7

Fashion Design and Product Development
Harold Carr & John Pomeroy
Sets out the modern, commercial approach and discusses practical factors including materials, manufacture, costs, quality and organisation of the process.

192 pages, illustrated paperback.
ISBN 0 632 02893 9

Fashion Marketing
Edited by Mike Easey
Marketing is now an indispensable component of fashion and clothing courses. This book satisfies students' requirements, and has a number of special qualities that make it essential reading for anyone in the business. Theory and practice are balanced, with examples to illustrate key concepts. Where numerical concepts are included, clear worked examples ensure that the ideas are easily understood and retained.
240 pages, illustrated paperbook.
0 632 03459 9

Introduction to Clothing Manufacture
Gerry Cooklin
This introductory textbook explains practical aspects of manufacture, from original design to deliveries to retailers; basic planning and manufacturing technologies; and contains realistic examples of the daily operations of a clothing factory.
190 pages, illustrated paperback.
ISBN 0 632 02661 8

Knitted Clothing Technology
Terry Brackenbury
Covers specific techniques used to convert weft knitted fabric into garments, techniques for shaping and construction, specialist assembly machinery, and future trends.
208 pages, illustrated paperbook.
ISBN 0 632 02807 6

CAD in Clothing and Textiles
Second Edition
Edited by Winifred Aldrich
With contributions from experts in the industry, this book discusses many aspects including writing software, sale of systems, applications, training and education.
224 pages, illustrated paperback.
ISBN 0 632 03893 4

Fabric, Form and Flat Pattern Cutting
Winifred Aldrich
The relationship between garment cut and fabric potential is probably the most important feature of present design skill. This book is based on an appraisal of the fabric and the body form to help students develop an intuitive and practical approach.
208 pages, illustrated paperback.

b
Blackwell
Science

A detailed catalogue with order form is available on request from:
Dept. CLO, Blackwell Science Ltd, Osney Mead, Oxford OX2 0EL, England.

Telephone 01865 206206 Fax 01865 721205